CROSSING THE BRIDGE

CROSSING THE BRIDGE: INTEGRATING SOLUTION FOCUSED THERAPY INTO CLINICAL PRACTICE

SUSAN LEE TOHN
AND
JORDAN A. OSHLAG

Solutions Press • Sudbury, Massachusetts

978

For sales contact Solutions Press: (508) 443-7574   Internet: SLTJAO@sprynet.com

Produced by: R.P.J. Associates
Printed in the United States of America

Library of Congress Cataloging-in-Publication Data

Tohn, Susan Lee, 1961-
      Crossing the Bridge: Integrating Solution Focused Therapy into
      Clinical Practice / by Susan Lee Tohn and Jordan A. Oshlag
      Includes bibliographical references and index.
      ISBN: 0-9648019-2-2
      Library of Congress Catalog Card Number: 95-74961
      1. Brief Therapy   2. Solution Focused Therapy   3. Psychotherapy, brief
      methods I. Oshlag, Jordan A. II. Title

Second Edition

Cover design by Rose DiSanto, DiSanto Design.

Dedicated to our daughters,
Helene and Elise

CONTENTS

The Authors

Susan Lee Tohn received her M.S.W. from Boston University School of Social Work. She is Co-Director of Solutions in Sudbury, Massachusetts. Ms. Tohn has worked extensively with couples, adolescents, and families using the Solution Focused model. She has provided training for and consulted with management teams, mental health organizations, hospitals, and managed care organizations, and has presented to professional audiences both nationally and internationally. Ms. Tohn is on the adjunct faculty at Boston University School of Social Work.

Jordan A. Oshlag received his M.S.W. from Boston University School of Social Work. He is Co-Director of Solutions in Sudbury, Massachusetts. Mr. Oshlag has had extensive experience working with adolescents and adult populations in a variety of settings. He has presented extensively to professional audiences and continues to train professionals in Solution Focused Brief Therapy both nationally and internationally. Mr. Oshlag is on the adjunct faculty at Boston University School of Social Work. In addition, Mr. Oshlag works for Hill Associates, a Healthcare Management Systems company as a clinical consultant, helping providers and agencies use the Hill Associates' Information System in clinical practice.

Solutions

Solutions is staffed by Susan Lee Tohn and Jordan A. Oshlag. Solutions' staff works with a wide variety of clientele and has many managed care contracts. The Solutions' staff utilizes a team approach when working with clients, which means clients receive the services of more than one therapist. The team consults with each other during the session and/or between sessions to provide the highest-quality treatment possible. Of course, all information is held in strict confidence. In addition, the staff presents workshops and seminars for agencies, hospitals, trade associations, and other organizations nationally and internationally.

To Contact the Authors or Solutions:

Solutions
243 Hudson Road
Sudbury, MA 01776-1624 USA

Phone and Fax: 508-443-7574
Internet: SLTJAO@sprynet.com

1

Introduction to Solution Focused Brief Therapy

There is nothing new about brief treatment. Most clinical programs have some course work on the various forms of brief treatment, and many trainees are exposed to the philosophies and assumptions of brief models of therapy. What is new is the demand on clinicians (read: generic term for mental health practitioner) to do brief therapy in a wide variety of clinical settings and with a variety of presenting problems. Most clinicians attend our workshops because they *need* to learn about brief/focused treatment, not because they *want* to.

Despite the fact that there is a huge demand for briefer work primarily due to the proliferation of managed behavioral health care, there has been very little discussion about becoming briefer in our work. The tools are presented and the demand clear; however, the guidance for how to *integrate* the concepts is too often missing. We make the assumption (among many) throughout this book that clinicians who learn to do more focused and briefer work will integrate the concepts into their existing clinical practice rather than becoming exclusively a Solution Focused therapist. When clinicians attempt to integrate the Solution Focused model into their clinical settings they are frustrated not because the techniques are too difficult, but because the systems in which clinicians work and the assumptions under which they work are not changing and adapting at the same pace as the clinicians. It appears counterproductive to have highly trained, focused clinicians working for an organization that demands a fourteen-page intake evaluation on every client. We are not, however, suggesting that there is no usefulness of such evaluations. We contend that they serve a different paradigm. Time and again we have consulted to systems needing to be overhauled to meet the demands of briefer work and to provide adequate support to clinicians.

Our goal in this book is to introduce the Solution Focused Brief Therapy model as we have utilized it, and discuss in detail the integration process. We have included sections in most chapters on integration issues. The reader will note that in Chapter 11 the integration issues are woven into the chapter. We would like to thank all the workshop participants over the years who have invited us to join them on their quest to integrate Solution Focused Brief Therapy into their clinical practice. In addition, we are deeply indebted to Dr. Scott Miller for his ongoing teaching and guidance, and Ms. Jean Holmblad for her patient editing and helpful suggestions. Most importantly we are indebted to our clients for teaching us how we can best help them help themselves.

We have tried to use unbiased language throughout this book. When we refer to clients in specific examples we do refer to them using the pronouns he or she. These are not intended to be representational of clients that present with any particular diagnosis or problem. We have also chosen to refer to all people that practice in the mental health field as clinicians or therapists. This term is used for convenience and not intended to exclude other helping professionals. All client names have been changed and identifying information altered, to preserve our clients' confidentiality.

Solution Focused Brief Therapy

Solution Focused Brief Therapy has been in existence for over twenty years. Steve deShazer is credited with beginning the model at the Brief Family Therapy Center in Milwaukee, Wisconsin. Many clinicians who have trained with deShazer and his partner, Insoo Kim Berg, have changed and adapted the model to fit their own assumptions and needs of practice. These include but are not limited to Dr. Scott Miller, Larry Hopwood, Michele Weiner-Davis, William O'Hanlon, Patricia Hudson, Yvonna Dolan, John Walter, Jane Peller, and others. There are several good resources that detail the development of Solution Focused Brief Therapy (deShazer, 1985, 1988, 1994; Berg & Miller, 1992; Hudson & Weiner-Davis, 1989). Readers can consult these resources for further information.

Solution Focused Therapy is not just long-term therapy done faster or in a shorter period of time; it is a different approach to working with clients. Most of the traditional forms of psychotherapy begin with the therapist developing a diagnosis, then treatment goals. This model, as we practice it, starts with the client and focuses on solutions. Our clients report to us that our work provides them with hope and control over the pace and focus of the treatment. We have found Solution Focused Therapy to be very respectful of cultural difference and variety of world views. The model has also helped us to treat each client as an individual and approach each new case with an open mind filled with wonderment. Another important aspect of the model is the ability for clients to measure, through the scaling questions, their own progress. It is wonderful in treatment when we recognize that our clients are improving, feeling and doing better; it is much more powerful when our clients recognize this in themselves. Solution Focused Therapy focuses on the present and future, utilizing the past as it is necessary. The model is non-pathology based. It is important to realize that the intent is to be solution focused, not brief. The fact that the work is briefer is an added benefit of being focused. It is important for us to emphasize that Solution Focused Therapy is not better or worse than any other form of treatment, in regard to treatment outcome and client satisfaction, although there has been very little research done in this area (Miller, 1993a). We do believe that what we do during a session is different; however, the results are not different (for further discussion see Miller, 1993a). We have found that some clinicians gravitate toward a Solution Focused approach and are able to successfully embrace the assumptions. The model does not work for everyone. Although the field of mental health is undergoing a dramatic change at this time this does not mean that this model is *the answer*. We encourage clinicians to study this model, evaluate it, and learn about a variety of brief therapies. As we are fond of saying in our trainings, if this were *the* model, we would all be doing it.

2

Assumptions of Solution Focused Brief Therapy

The assumptions that we hold about our work and our clients drive the type of clinical work that we do. By assumptions we mean our thoughts, feelings, values, and attitudes that affect our work with clients. As Moshe Talmon points out, "Therapists' attitudes are critical to the way they operate, think, and feel in the process of psychotherapy" (Talmon, 1990). Our assumptions are a guiding force in the work we do and influence both us and our clients. As deShazer, et al (1986) stated:

> Therapists need to make some assumptions about the construction of complaints and the nature of solutions in order to do their job. (Although our assumptions are somewhat idiosyncratic...) Let's say that the therapist assumes that "symptoms" have a systemic function – they hold the family together. In this case he or she will draw a map that suggests how that function can be served in that

system without the symptom. (Brief Therapy: Family
Process, p. 210)

How do we decide which assumptions are *right for us* given all of the
different theoretical perspectives which appear to be equally valid and
helpful to the client? An exploration of the general influence, creation,
and maintenance of our assumptions is a good place to begin.

As therapists, we use the therapeutic interview as our
intervention. The relationship and interaction between client and therapist
is paramount. Therefore *what* we ask during the interaction becomes
crucial since our questions are how we operationalize our intervention.
All therapists accomplish three tasks during a session regardless of one's
therapeutic orientation. We elicit, amplify, and reinforce information
(thoughts, beliefs, values, feelings, behaviors). What we choose to elicit,
amplify, and reinforce varies greatly, and consequently, the information
we obtain will vary. If we walk into a room and start a conversation
about fly-fishing (even though we know nothing about it), in some manner
or another we are going to be talking about fly-fishing. Similarly, if we
ask clients about problems [solutions, history, their mother], we are going
to engage in a conversation about problems. It has typically been our
experience that clients will follow our lead in an effort to cooperate with
us (Berg & Miller, 1992). Therefore it is crucial for us to be cognizant
that whatever we ask about becomes the focus and direction of the
therapeutic encounter.

Sources of Assumptions

If assumptions are paramount to our work, where do they come
from? People go into the therapy field with a portion of their assumptions
already in place, while others are acquired. A therapist's prior experience
doing counseling, giving advice, solving problems, and being a client can
influence his/her assumptions. During a professional's training
assumptions are rarely discussed directly – ours or our clients'. On the
basis of our training, some assumptions we have believed and many of our
trainees have talked about are: *Clients need help; we can provide help;
some people need more help than others; take nothing at face value,*

there is an underlying reason for the problems you are seeing and your job is to find it; there are some people who have a high level of insight and some who don't; some people are more ready and willing to be in therapy than others; think systemically; and more. This list is not completely conscious, and it is definitely not stagnant.

In the past, depending on the client, insurance company, presenting problem, supervisor, agency, mood, weather, and what training we had most recently been to, our assumptions would fluctuate above and below the conscious level. Most influential was *the diagnosis;* we believed this would somehow indicate a treatment direction. If we could accurately diagnosis *the problem,* then we could find *the answer* and supposedly know what we should be doing while sitting across from our clients. In practice however, this is not always the case. Assumptions about our work and our clients tie in closely with our values and the nature of the work we do (Miller, 1993b). Our beliefs are based on our subjective thinking. Given that there is little if any empirical evidence to suggest that one type of treatment is any better than another (Miller, 1993a), clinicians should at least be aware of our own assumptions that lead us to do a certain style of counseling.

During the many trainings we conduct we spend considerable time asking trainees to explore their assumptions. The process usually starts off slowly; people are either shy or unsure about articulating their assumptions. For many this is the first time that they have been asked to explore their assumptions. It is important to emphasize that assumptions are not wrong or right, they just are. For example, one assumption that we hold is that "it is unnecessary to know a lot about the problem in order to resolve it" (deShazer, 1988). Another therapist may hold the assumption that he/she needs to know a lot about the problem in order to resolve it. Both of these assumptions are valid in our opinion. Depending on which assumption you hold, it is our contention that you will ask very different questions, you will get different answers, and treatment will move along in different directions. For example, if we assume people have the strengths and resources to solve their own problems (Rabkin, 1983; O'Hanlon & Wilk, 1987; O'Hanlon & Weiner-Davis, 1989), we might ask, "How did you solve this the last time?"

In an effort to clarify our assumptions it has been helpful to ask ourselves what assumption a question is based on, and then work backwards to the basis of that question. For example, if we ask a client "How can I help you solve your problem?" We are assuming that (1) we can help the client, (2) there is a problem, and (3) the client wants our help with this problem. In addition, when we hear an assumption that we do not agree with we ask ourselves what assumption we believe, and we will often ask the same question of our colleagues. Very often during team meetings with five therapists in the room, we will have seven opinions. We believe this is caused primarily by our different assumptions. We feel that it is important to be aware of our assumptions for several reasons. Doing therapy has never been, and will most likely never be, an exact science. In an effort to be as consistent as possible, we have found that having a clear understanding of the forces that drive our work is a key step. The more consistent we are in our work, the better we are able to evaluate its effectiveness. In addition, knowing our current assumptions allows us to better evaluate new models of treatment, new techniques, and the assumptions on which they are based.

Maintenance of Assumptions

The first step in changing our assumptions was to explore them. The easiest way for us to do this was to think about our assumptions and have several different sets of assumptions clearly defined for us. As we learned about the assumptions of Solution Focused Brief Therapy (deShazer, 1985, 1988; deShazer, Berg, Lipchik, Nunnally, Molnar, Gingerich, & Weiner-Davis, 1986), we were able to compare and contrast these assumptions with our own as we became aware of them. Even if we did not agree, we were still able to ask ourselves what assumption we did believe, where had it come from, and did it "fit" well with who we were as clinical social workers at that time. This exploration (questioning) was a very uncomfortable endeavor. It took many conversations with other clinicians who were thinking about the current trends in mental health to sort out our assumptions and to identify their origins.

Knowing what assumptions we believe can help us in our work. Talmon (1990) refers to assumptions as attitudes. He states, "Attitudes play a *central* role (emphasis added) in all forms of psychotherapy. Evidently, therapists' attitudes are expressed in their first questions in the initial session." In our work one of the first questions we ask our clients is, "What brings you here today?" This question is based on our assumption, and the assumption of Solution Focused Brief Therapy, that clients set the goals of treatment (O'Hanlon & Weiner-Davis, 1989). By believing that clients should set the goals, we can then formulate logical and consistent questions based on this assumption. We often get asked by clinicians who observe a Solution Focused session, "How did you know to ask that question?" The answer is that we base our questions on our assumptions, and since we are clear what our assumptions are, it becomes easier to know what question to ask next.

As mental health services continue to undergo radical changes in the era of managed mental health, therapists will be challenged to continually adapt to new settings, rules, requirements, and therapy techniques. In an effort to acclimate to these changes, new techniques that arise, or old ones making a resurgence, it is vital to be cognizant of our assumptions. As we are called upon to change, knowing where we are coming from becomes even more important to help us get to where we want to go.

Assumptions of Solution Focused Brief Therapy

What follows are the Solution Focused assumptions as we interpret them. These are similar to other explanations of the Solution Focused assumptions (deShazer, 1985, 1988; Berg & Miller 1992; O'Hanlon & Weiner-Davis, 1989; Walter & Peller, 1992) and have been expanded and interpreted to fit our view of the model It is not necessary to believe all of the assumptions in order to practice Solution Focused Therapy. All of the questions we ask in a session are based on at least one of these assumptions. If you do not agree with one of these assumptions, we encourage you to ask yourself what assumption you do hold that makes it so you cannot accept this Solution Focused assumption.

If it works, do it more

This assumption applies to both the therapist and the client. With respect to the therapist, if we are working with clients who are reporting progress toward their goals, we continue to do what we are doing. The key point is progress toward the *clients' goals*, not the therapist's, agency's, or society's goals; even though the clients' solution may not be the one the therapist would prefer, this assumption encourages the therapist to tell the client to do it more. This helps the client to build patterns of success. It is important to highlight these patterns, and not suggest "better" solutions, which can confuse and disempower the client.

Sometimes, clients are not aware of their own progress. This is a time when the therapist's skills of amplification and reinforcement are crucial. Many times, if you ask clients about pre-session change (Weiner-Davis, deShazer, & Gingerish, 1987), they will report progress toward their goals. As illustrated by a study conducted at The Brief Family Therapy Center in Milwaukee, Wisconsin, in 1987 (Weiner-Davis, deShazer, & Gingerish, 1987), when clients were asked about change even before therapy began, many reported positive change. Weiner-Davis asked each client coming in for therapy, "Many times people notice in between the time they make the appointment for therapy and the first session that things already seem different. What have you noticed about your situation?...Are these the kinds of changes you would like to continue to have happen?" (Weiner-Davis, deShazer, & Gingerish, p. 360). Sixty-six percent of the sample reported that they had noticed some difference. If expanded beyond the scope of this research, the potential exists that for two out of three clients coming to see us, they are already doing something to improve their situation! Although this is not "fact," it is intriguing to entertain this thought when seeing clients for the first time.

If it is not broken, don't fix it

Solution Focused clinicians work hard to cooperate with clients. Part of this cooperation involves allowing clients the autonomy to decide what goals they want to work on with us in therapy. It is important to remember that as therapists we have several roles in society that at first glance may seem to contradict or be in direct conflict with this assumption. We view mandated reporting of such issues as sexual abuse of children and the threat of harm to self or others (or other mandating categories in your state) to be separate from "therapy," and we think of them as social control functions which are also a part of our job (Dawes, 1994).

This assumption creates a great deal of respect for our clients and encourages client self-determination. It also helps us to be sensitive to, and respectful of, cultural differences among our clients, and between ourselves and our clients. We are also careful not to add problems to our clients' list. This is sometimes very challenging, particularly when we recognize issues that we are trained to notice. For example, when a client presents with "communication" issues in a marriage and we suspect the client may have a drinking problem, we begin by agreeing with the client's view of the world, and at that time do not confront the client about the suspected drinking. What makes following this assumption easier is the next assumption.

Clients have the resources and strengths to resolve their complaints

One of the most difficult assumptions for us to adopt, having been trained in a psychodynamically oriented model, was that clients have the resources and strengths to resolve their complaints. Solution Focused Brief Therapy truly believes that clients are their own best experts. Oftentimes people confuse this assumption and do not allow others in the clients' system to help them fix the problem. Family members, others in a therapeutic milieu, and group members can help form a solution; the key is that the onus is not on the therapist. Putting this into practice is easier said than done. We utilize the Solution Focused technique of looking for exceptions to help us in this endeavor (see Chapter 7). Sometimes clients will come up with a solution that we would not choose, or one that would not work for us. The assumption that clients have their own resources allows us to encourage clients' self-determination. In order to truly let clients decide what they will and will not discuss in therapy, the clinician has to believe that clients know what is best for them and that they possess the resources to accomplish their goals. If clinicians believe this assumption, then there is no resistance or denial (deShazer, 1989). In our experience resistance and denial tend to occur when the therapist or other people try to convince clients they have a problem. When other people (partners, protective service workers, courts) impose goals on clients, we focus on cooperating with our clients (see Chapter 3). This assumption also frees the therapist from having to "fix" clients or the clients' problems. The responsibility remains with clients, since it is their goal.

Returning to the communication/drinking example: Once we have agreed with the client that improving communication is the goal, one of two things will happen. Either the client will return and report progress with communication, or she will not. When the client reports progress, this means that she did not need to discuss her drinking with us in order to begin to solve this problem. The possibility exists that she did not address the issue of drinking at all, or dealt with it on her own. If however, the client returns and reports no progress with communication, then we take the opportunity to "be dumb" and ask, "What else do you think we need to work on?" However, when the client reports no progress, we are often tempted to start analyzing "the problem." It is important not to bite the apple! What we have found most beneficial is to remind ourselves of another assumption, which is that **clients want to solve their problems.** Based on this assumption our effort is then to redirect the client toward her solution to the problem, rather than discussing the problem in more detail. Another aspect of our assumptions is that we believe we must have excellent rapport with our clients before we can begin to challenge any of their beliefs. If the client continues to report no progress toward her goals, we may, at some point, challenge her beliefs in an effort to get her unstuck. We believe that helping clients to "get on track to solving their problems," (Walter & Peller, 1992) is often good enough for the clients. Many clients do not need our help after this. We have often had clients call us after one or two sessions and tell us, "I've got it, thanks."

If it does not work, try something else

As therapists we must decide at what point we are going to say to ourselves that our client is not progressing and we need to try something else. At our practice, we start asking ourselves this question by the second or third session if the client is reporting that there is no progress. There is no need repeating what did not work. Oftentimes in the past we would assign the same homework task again and again because we did not get the results we wanted. Now, we will try many things that appear subtle, but are different:

- Listen better
- Re-examine the goals
- Change rooms
- Use a team
- Do not use a team
- Change therapist

When clients report that things are not better, we also challenge them to do something different. At times our clients are so frustrated or stuck that we may need to help them create new ideas about what they can do differently. Another possibility is that our clients holds a belief that prevents progress. Our job then is to challenge this belief and help our clients to create a new belief that will lead to a new set of solutions. For example, we worked with a woman who was dealing with issues of sexual abuse, and she believed that she must confront her abuser. This was an extremely anxiety provoking thought for her, and so she could not do it and reported no progress. By the third session we decided to challenge this belief and asked her how she knew that confronting her abuser would be helpful to her. She said that a TV talk show host suggested this during a special program on abuse. She also believed that if she could confront her abuser he would apologize and ask her forgiveness. As we explored this scenario, she quickly realized that he probably would not admit he had done anything wrong nor apologize, and that she did run the risk of being hurt further emotionally. Once she thought it through she decided on a different course of action that produced positive results by the next session as demonstrated by the following case example.

> *THERAPIST*: So what do you think your next step is?
>
> *CLIENT*: I think I have to confront my abuser.
>
> *THERAPIST*: So when you confront your abuser, what will be different?
>
> *CLIENT*: I can tell him how I was affected by what he did to me.
>
> *THERAPIST*: And once you have been able to do this, how will this be helpful to you?
>
> *CLIENT*: What do you mean?
>
> *THERAPIST*: What do you believe will be the result of telling him how you have been effected by the abuse?
>
> *CLIENT*: He'll say he is sorry and get some help.
>
> *THERAPIST:* And how do you know that's what will happen? *(This is an example of challenging a client's belief system in order to get her unstuck).*
>
> *CLIENT:* Well, I guess I don't....I wish that is what he would say...but considering who he is and his record, I guess it's unrealistic to think he would suddenly just be sorry when I bring it up.
>
> *THERAPIST*: So in thinking about the possible responses he can choose to give when you confront him, are there other ways you can get what you need without depending on him to respond in a certain way?
>
> *CLIENT:* Well I'm not sure what that is.
>
> *THERAPIST:* Well, It's something to think about...(*once we have challenged a belief we may not push at that time to create a new belief. We have found that clients will think about it and make the shift when they are ready*). Okay, what else would be different for you once you have confronted him.
>
> *CLIENT*: I'll be able to get on with my life.

THERAPIST: Oh, so you would be able to get on with your life? When you know you are getting on with your life what will be different for you?

CLIENT: You know, I just had this thought, maybe what I need to do is just accept that he is never going to change, and never going to say he is sorry.

THERAPIST: Maybe. What would it take for you to do that?

CLIENT: I guess if I could get on with my life, then it would not matter if he said he was sorry. I just always thought that he needed to say he was sorry first. Maybe that is not true.

Change is constant

A woman approached Susan during the second installment of a training several years back and stated that she had gone home, and really watched her children. She reported that they were truly changing all the time, but she had not been looking for it! Our clients, and people in general, make attempts to solve problems and do something different all the time. The trouble begins when this difference is not noticed by the client or others in the world. We have worked with many adolescents with school problems who tell us that they really have tried during the previous two weeks to improve their behavior, but nothing is different. When we question the parents and teachers, it does not take long to discover that no one has noticed. We believe that looking for change is as important as doing something different.

We also find that few, if any, therapists actively and consistently ask about change, especially positive change. Our clients learn early on that we expect that things will get better, and that we ask during each session "what is better." We believe it is important to distinguish between actively pursuing positive change and becoming what Nylund and Corsiglia (1994) call *"solution-forced"* or what Dr. Scott Miller (1993b) calls *"problem phobic."* Although we want our clients to realize that positive change should occur in therapy, we do not want them to color the truth and not tell us when things are not getting better or are getting worse. Many times it is a matter of allowing clients to direct the session.

Case Example: Carla is a 35-year-old married woman with two children. She had originally come to therapy for depression. Over the course of treatment Carla had worked very hard and had made great strides in her life. Below is an excerpt of one of our last sessions.

> *THERAPIST*: So, what's been better since we met last?
> *CARLA*: Well, some things have been much better, but I
>   really need to discuss something with you.
> *THERAPIST*: Okay, which would you like to do first?
> *CARLA*: I definitely need to start with what happened this
>   week.
> *THERAPIST*: Okay, what happened?
> *CARLA*: Well, my grandmother died last week and.....

Carla spent much of the session telling me about the loss of her grandmother and discussing how she had dealt with the situation. Toward the end of the session she said:

> Oh, by the way, remember at the beginning I told you that
>   things were better? Well, I went on a job
>   interview this week (*a longtime goal of hers*).

Successful treatment includes listening to clients and moving with them as they are ready to move.

The therapist's job is to identify and amplify change
It is usually unnecessary to know a great deal about the complaint in
order to resolve it

It is our belief that all therapists, by the nature of their work, ask questions that identify and amplify information. In our view what information you choose to amplify is important and should be a conscious decision. During our workshops we often have participants practice the beginning portions of a first interview. During these practice sessions we instruct participants *not* to inquire about "the problem" but rather to just start with a future-based question such as the Miracle Question (see Chapter 6). Participants are continually amazed that clients (and therapists) can begin to discuss what the client wants, without ever hearing about what the client does not want. Solution Focused Therapy has no "tip of the iceberg" theory (Fischer, 1984; Berg & Miller, 1992) that assumes that the problem as we see it is only the beginning and we must dig to find the rest.

It is not necessary to know the cause or function of a complaint to resolve it

One result of pop psychology is that many clients believe the therapist needs to know the cause of their problem in order to help. This notion comes directly from the medical model and has permeated therapists' assumptions also. When we take our car to the garage, we do not need the mechanic to spend forty minutes explaining to us why our car will not start. What we need is for her to fix it. Although the analogy is not perfect, we do not assume that clients need us to explain their problems. We have found that there is a distinct difference between what people tell us is wrong, and what they want. In fact, many times these two are not as related as we might assume. As you will see when we discuss first sessions, it is important to allow clients to tell their story, but this is for their benefit, not ours; however, their story may be a good source for gathering information which may help you fill out forms and billing – two events we distinguish from doing therapy. For example, when clients come in and say they are depressed, we would ask the following:

> *CLIENT*: I'm depressed and I need to know why.
> *THERAPIST*: If you were no longer depressed, but you never knew why, would this be good enough?

Most clients tell us that it would be good enough to just not be depressed anymore. Those who say no, it would not be good enough (many of whom are therapists themselves), have a very legitimate reason. If they do not know why they were depressed in the first place, they are concerned it will happen again, even if they stop being depressed for a while. In this case, it is the clients' need to explore they are depressed. With clients who have this need, we will begin by asking them their theories about why they are depressed. These typically range in number from one to five reasons (depending on whether they have been in therapy before and how long they have been depressed). We have yet to meet a client who has no explanations. We work to validate their explanations (see below). The exception to this assumption is when we feel that a client's explanation is self-destructive or bizarre thinking. In these cases we would challenge these beliefs and ask questions to elicit alternative explanations. This assumption contradicts a long-term insight-oriented therapy assumption that *insight leads to change*.

There is no one right way to view things;
different views may be just as valid and may fit the facts just as well

When clients give an explanation for why things are the way that they are, we accept it, with the exceptions noted above. Although our explanations usually fit our world view better and are based on experience and clinical training, they do not necessarily fit our clients' world view better than their own. As deShazer (1994) so adeptly points out, our job is to read the lines, not between the lines. After fully validating our clients' view of the world, regardless of their explanations, our question is the same: "Now that you know why, what is it that you would like to be different?"

A small change is all that is needed
A change in one part of the system can
effect a change in another part

The systemic view that no part of a system can go unchanged without affecting other parts of the system is a popular belief in systemic thinking (Berg & Miller, 1992; Rossi, 1973). Our job as therapists is to look for small change, and to train our clients to look for the small change.Many people whom we counsel can articulate what they want – their goals. Few however, bother to break this goal down into small, doable, well-formed goals (see Chapter 4). We have found some (mostly male) clients are big idea people, but they can't tell the trees from the forest. Breaking every goal down into small parts is essential to the goal's success.

> *CLIENT*: I want to be able to communicate better with my wife.
>
> *THERAPIST*: What will be the first signs to you that you are beginning to communicate better?
>
> *CLIENT*: I don't know...If we talked more.
>
> *THERAPIST*: And what would be the first step toward the two of you talking more?
>
> *CLIENT*: I guess we would need to spend some time together.
>
> *THERAPIST*: And what would it take for that to happen?...

Clients learn through the therapy process to examine their own goals and to break them down into small, doable pieces. Once they accomplish the first small goal, they are usually more confident they can achieve other goals.

Clients define the goals

Although it may seem obvious, Solution Focused Therapy emphasizes working on those goals that clients identify as important. This can become challenging when clients think someone else needs to change, or that there is no problem to be worked on (see Chapter 5). We have found Solution Focused Therapy particularly useful when dealing with these clients, as we will discuss in more detail later (see Chapter 3).

Rapid change or resolution of problems is possible

Moshe Talmon advises:

Most therapists, including myself, have been trained to view psychotherapy as a relatively long process, ranging from a few months to lifelong affairs. Viewing the first session only as a time for assessment is just one example of a fragmented attitude toward the nature of psychotherapy and the therapist's role in it...Taking each session one at a time and treating it as a whole can help the therapist to make use of the present without fearing the future. It encourages both client and therapist to do something about the problem without large expenses and dependency. (Talmon, 1990, pp. 117-118)

When we approach every session as if it may be the only contact we are going to have with that client, we believe our frame of reference to be altered from that of traditional therapy. In our practice we examine those cases that appear to be unplanned terminations. When clients do not return many therapists assume that this is an indication of treatment failure. We encourage therapists to call clients and inquire as to why they decided to discontinue therapy. Many times clients report that they received what they came for, and they no longer need our services. This can hardly be regarded as treatment failure!

Focus on what is possible and changeable
rather than what is impossible and intractable

O'Hanlon and Weiner-Davis (1989) and Friedman and Fanger (1991) emphasize the importance of focusing the work on those goals that are possible and changeable. Regardless of the type of therapy you are practicing, it is important to have well-formed goals. We discuss this in further detail in Chapter 4.

You get what you ask for

In our minds the most important assumption to remember is that you get what you ask for. When we enter a room and begin to discuss fly-fishing, we have some conversation about fly-fishing, despite the fact that no one in the room knows anything about fly-fishing. Similarly, when we inquire about clients' depression (problems), we are subtly and not so subtly sending the message that talking about problems is essential in order to help clients reach their goals. Depending on your therapeutic orientation, this may very well be the case. Our belief is that therapists should be keenly aware of what they are asking and the influence of their words. In order to operate therapeutically within these assumptions it is vital for us to think carefully about the questions we ask our clients, because our questions are our interventions. The litmus test we conduct on each question is, "Is the question I am about to ask going to help the client meet her goal, or make progress toward her goal?" If we are uncertain, or certain that the question will not help the client toward her goal, we refrain from asking. This is sometimes very difficult! Scott Miller tells the story of a workshop participant asking him, "What happens when you know that the question will not help the client reach her goal, but you really need to ask it? What do you do?" Scott replied, "Go home, lie down, and wait for the feeling to go away" (Miller, 1993b).

INTEGRATION ISSUES

Integrating assumptions. The assumptions from this chapter with which you agree will either already be a part of your clinical work or will easily be integrated into your work. You will find that the Solution Focused questions that originate from that particular assumption are not so difficult to remember.

Assumptions that challenge you. When thinking about the assumptions from this chapter with which you cannot agree or are not sure where you stand, we encourage you to think about your assumption that makes it difficult to agree with the Solution Focused assumption. What you will find is that these assumptions will be the most challenging for you when it comes to asking Solution Focused questions. One experiment to try is to pretend you believe a specific assumption and experience what it is like to ask questions based on that assumption. This is a challenging way to work with clients and may take some practice before you feel comfortable. Another suggestion is to videotape a session and then review your questions and how they might shift if you changed some of your assumptions.

Why is it briefer? Although not the original intention, Solution Focused Therapy has been marketed as brief therapy. We have found that one explanation for this can be found with the assumption, "The therapist's job is to identify and amplify change. It is usually unnecessary to know a great deal about the complaint in order to resolve it," and also the assumption, "It is not necessary to know the cause or function of a complaint to resolve it." If you do not assume clients need to tell you their history or explore the causes of their problem, you can potentially save a large number of sessions. The exception, of course, is when clients say they need to tell us this information in order to move on.

3

Cooperating with Clients

Based on the assumptions discussed, we have found that the best way to "meet clients where they are" is to learn to cooperate with them. By cooperation we mean to believe and function as if the client's view of the world makes sense and is correct, and to communicate that we respect that view. This may seem contrary to our professional training, which teaches us to be "the experts." By cooperating with our clients in this manner we are stating that they are the experts on their lives, and we must do everything we can to learn from them (Berg & Miller, 1992). When thinking about diversity and working with clients from a different culture, this paradigm steers us toward being nonjudgmental. A helpful technique in this pursuit is to classify the relationship between the Client, Therapist, and Problem/Goal into three distinct triads: customer-seller, complainant-listener, and visitor-host type relationship (Berg & Miller, 1992; deShazer, 1988). These triads refer to the relationship among the three components and are *not* intended as labels for clients. Assessing which relationship a client is in, at any given time, for any given problem and any goal, can help us determine what role the therapist should take in the session. It is important to remember that we do not try to shift clients from one relationship to the other; we are not in the convincing business. Rather we work with our clients, from their view of the world, within the parameters of the clients' relationship to the problem and particular goal.

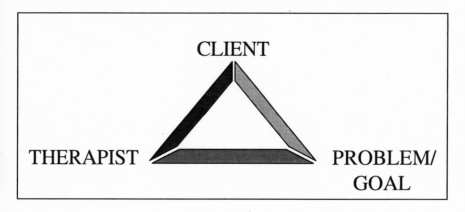

The Customer-Seller Type Relationship

In this relationship clients are the customers, and therapists are the sellers. As customers clients give details about the problem, state that they are part of the problem, and part of the solution. Clients take some if not all responsibility for doing something about the problem. Clients in this relationship often say things like, "I have a drinking problem and I need to do something about it," or "I need to learn ways to be less stressed." The therapist's job is to help these clients reach their goals; in other words, to be a good salesperson. This can appear deceptively easy to do. For example, if a customer were to enter a popular electronics store and tell the .eager salesperson he was having trouble playing tapes on his VCR, the conversation might go like this:

> *Customer*: Every time I turn on the TV and play a tape I
> get these fuzzy lines all over the TV screen.
> *Salesperson*: How long has this been a problem?

Customer: Two weeks.
Salesperson: What would you like from us today?
Customer: Well, I think a new TV will do the trick.

At this point the salesperson has to decide if she is going to cooperate with the customer or add her opinion to the conversation.

Cooperating with the client	Not cooperating with the client
Salesperson: Let me show you where we keep the TVs. *Customer*: Great. *Salesperson*: Now if this does not clear up the problem, please be sure to come back and we will try to figure out what else it could be. *Customer*: Great, I will.	*Salesperson*: Well, I do not think that it is the TV, I am sure that your problem is your VCR, so you should buy a new VCR. *Customer*: I don't think I have a problem with my VCR. *Salesperson*: Well, if you do not buy a VCR, I am afraid this problem will only get worse.

Now, one of two things will happen. Either the customer was right and the new TV will fix the problem, or he was wrong. In the event that he was wrong, he will return and the salesperson will then get to suggest working on the VCR. When we do not cooperate with our clients we impose our own definition of the problem, potential solutions, and potentially other problems onto our clients.

When this conversation is applied to the area of substance abuse, it is easy to see how complicated matters can become. When we do not cooperate with our clients, we end up confronting them and trying to convince them that alcohol is the problem. The paradigm shift discussed earlier allows us to concentrate on what clients want, not what we believe clients need to do to solve their problems. Just as we will soon ask our clients to suspend for a moment how they are going to solve their problems when we ask the Miracle Question, we must also suspend our assumptions about "how" clients will solve their problems and first discover "what" clients want. What we have found over and over again is that when we cooperate with our clients by asking them what they want, they are much more likely to find the solution that works for them faster than if we were to impose our methods of fixing problems on them. Even in the case of clients who are abusing alcohol and other drugs, we address these issues if they are central to achieving their goal (Berg & Miller, 1992).

The Complainant-Listener Type Relationship

In this relationship clients can tell the therapist a lot about the problem; how it started, who is involved, what keeps it going, and who has tried what to fix it. However, someone or something else must change first, before these clients can reach their goal(s). As Berg and Miller (1992) describe it, "The therapist agrees to explore the complaint or goal further with the client and to do so in a way that is intended to facilitate a new perspective that might lead to a solution." The therapist's role in this relationship is to work with our clients, challenge their beliefs when appropriate, and work toward the clients' goals. A prime example of this relationship is described by the dialogue below:

> *THERAPIST*: So your son has been having school problems?
>
> *CLIENT*: Yes, I just wish he would get up, go to school on his own, and stop messing up in class. He has always had trouble in school, since I can remember. He has always gotten extra help in school but it does not seem to be working. My husband and I have tried everything; it is up to him at this point.

Over the years it has been our experience that these are the clients with whom it is most difficult to work. Many times we become frustrated with clients who blame others for their troubles, labeling these clients as resistant, in denial, or severely disturbed. Using the complainant-listener paradigm allows us to concentrate on our clients and not try to convince them to focus on the issues we or others may perceive as the "real" problem. Oftentimes we find that the client in the complainant-listener type relationship ends up stuck in a box.

THE BOX

PROBLEM	*PROPOSED SOLUTION*	*GOAL*
	GO TO SCHOOL	

Suppose a client comes in stating that there is a particular problem such as in the school example above. The problem as she sees it is that he is doing poorly in school. The "solution" to her problem is that he "get up, go to school on his own, and stop messing up in class." If we take this as the "solution" or goal, we will be working on a goal that is poorly formed. We, however, assume that in this case, the "solution" that the client has proposed is *how* the problem can be solved, not *what will be different* when the problem is solved. The key is to inquire what will be different once the solution is successful and we ask this by incorporating the client's proposed solution into our next question.

> *THERAPIST*: So when your son is able to go to school, what will be different?
> *CLIENT*: He won't be in as much trouble and will get better grades. We will not get as many calls from the school.

THERAPIST: What else will be different when all that
            happens?
CLIENT: I guess we will not worry about his future as
         much and know that we can begin to trust him
         again.

The purpose of these questions is to help clients move around the box and start to articulate their goals, not how they are going to reach these goals. Our assumption is that the proposed "how" has not worked, or only worked to a degree. In addition, care must be taken not to land in yet another box.

THERAPIST: So when your son is able to go to school,
            what will be different? (*Box 1*)
CLIENT: He won't be in as much trouble and will get
         better grades. We will not get as many calls from
         the school.
THERAPIST: What else will be different when all that
            happens?
CLIENT: I'll know that his self-esteem is higher. (*Box 2*)

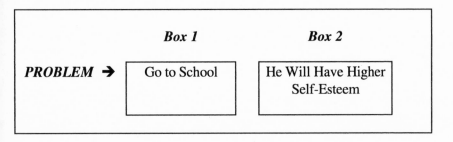

Having "higher self-esteem" is not a well-formed goal. We utilize the same incorporation technique to get a well-formed goal from the client.

THERAPIST: So when your son has higher self-esteem,
            what will be different?

CLIENT: Well, he will like himself more, he will do more things like socialize, and he will talk more to me, tell me what is going on in his life.

THERAPIST: What difference will this make in the problems that brought you in today?

CLIENT: I will trust him more.

Another advantage of this line of questioning is that we get to further understand our clients' definitions of the language they use. In addition, clients often glean new information from their answers to these questions. In the above case the son sitting in the room hears for the first time that his mother would trust him more if he tells her more.

In some cases, secondary problems are created by the attempted "solution." In the example illustrated in the box below, the wife's attempt at solving her husband's problem has created a second problem, which is viewed as primary by the husband (Watzlawick, P. Weakland, J., and Fisch, R., 1974). The wife's proposed solution of trying to convince the husband to stop drinking creates a new problem for the husband and one that he can focus on instead of dealing with his drinking.

Problem 1	*Proposed Solution*	*Goal*
He is never home	Husband stop drinking	

Problem 2 She nags me about my drinking

There is one other advantage to this type of questioning when a clients begin by stating that others will change. Now and then clients will discover that they can begin to work on achieving their goals despite the fact that someone else is the problem.

> *THERAPIST*: What brings you here today?
>
> *CLIENT*: My son is driving me nuts. He really needs your help. I am very worried about him.
>
> *THERAPIST*: How is he driving you nuts?
>
> *CLIENT*: I just want him to get a haircut, stop listening to that damn music, and hangout with kids who can spell their own name!
>
> *THERAPIST*: So when your son gets a haircut and does these other things, what will be different?
>
> *CLIENT*: His grades will go up. I'll know where he is more of the time.
>
> *THERAPIST*: And when you know that, what will be different for you?
>
> *CLIENT*: I guess I would not worry as much.
>
> *THERAPIST*: That's right. And when you are not worrying as much, what else will be different for you?
>
> *CLIENT*: I won't have this tightness in my chest all the time. The doctor won't have to give me Xanax; I'll just feel better.

At the end of this exchange the client is beginning to identify goals for herself. By continuing this type of questioning the client soon realizes that she can effect her "anxiety" whether or not her son is in counseling.

Visitor-Host Type Relationship

In this relationship clients do not feel they have a problem and therefore have no goals for treatment. These clients see no reason for change. The therapist's role is to make clients in the visitor-host type relationship (to a particular goal) feel comfortable and not try to convince them that a problem really does exist. More often than not these clients have been confronted by several people about the "problem" prior to reaching our office. It serves no purpose to be the next person in the same line. Since there is no goal in these clients' minds, it would not make sense to pursue any goal. It is rare for clients to remain true visitors for a specific goal when we cooperate with their view of the world and accept their view as legitimate.

> *THERAPIST*: What brings you here today?
> *CLIENT*: I don't want to be here.
> *THERAPIST*: Okay.
> *CLIENT*: The Department of Social Services said if I ever wanted to get my kids back I had to get counseling.
> *THERAPIST*: What would you like to get by coming here?
> *CLIENT*: Honestly?
> *THERAPIST*: Sure.
> *CLIENT*: I want you, DSS, and everybody who looks like you to get out of my face, and leave me and my family alone.

At this point it could easily be assumed that this client is in the visitor relationship, not really willing to work on anything. However, we view this client in the customer-seller type relationship rather than in the visitor-host type relationship. The goal of "getting everyone who looks like you out of my face" is a goal!

> *THERAPIST*: That sounds good to me. What do you think would need to happen for me and DSS to get out of your face and leave you alone?
> *CLIENT*: (*Smile, pause*) They (DSS) would have to know I'm not going to beat my kids anymore.
> *THERAPIST*: What do you think they would need to notice you doing differently to convince them of that?

The process of finding the goals that clients are willing to work on begins by assuming that our clients know what is best for themselves. More often than not clients end up working on those goals that "society" has deemed important, but they are doing it for their own reasons, not society's. This eliminates most cases of resistance and denial. Clients can only resist a goal imposed by someone else.

In the event that a client truly is in the visitor relationship for all goals, the task of the therapist is to make that person comfortable, and invite the client to return. From our experience a true visitor will either be able to negotiate a goal, or will not return.

To complicate the process, more often than not we find that people are in different relationships with various problems or goals. For example, a mother brought in her adolescent daughter because she had been told she had an eating disorder. The mother already had the daughter seeing a doctor and a nutritionist. After working with them for a few sessions without much progress, we finally realized our error. We had assumed the daughter was in the visitor relationship because she kept saying she did not have an eating disorder. The shift in treatment occurred when we began to examine this more closely. What we discovered was that the daughter was in the visitor-host relationship for the eating disorder, but was in the customer-seller relationship for getting her mom off her back. The mother was in the complainant-listener relationship for convincing her daughter she had an eating disorder. Once we realized the daughter was in the customer-seller type relationship, we gave her and her mother tasks that began to move things forward (see diagram below).

GOAL		TRIAD RELATIONSHIP
Daughter Has An Eating Disorder	➜	Mother: Complainant-Listener
		Daughter: Visitor-Host
Get Mother Off Daughter's Back	➜	Mother: Complainant-Listener
		Daughter: Customer-Seller

THE BOX

Problem	Proposed Solution	Goals
Woman doesn't get along with parents, which triggers eating disorder behavior	Talk with partner and develop plan on the car ride over	Know she is handling situation with parents in a good way as measured by healthy eating behavior

---

Case Example: The client reported that when she goes to her parents for a visit she gets so anxious that she regresses into bingeing behavior, which then disrupts what is usually a good week. We explore what she wants to be different about this situation.

> THERAPIST: So when you go to your parents you always end up bingeing?
>
> CLIENT: Yep. It is so frustrating, and my partner doesn't understand and doesn't seem able to help me with this.
>
> THERAPIST: Okay, are there any times when you are able to go to your parents and not end up bingeing (*we are looking for exceptions here*)?
>
> CLIENT: No, it always happens.
>
> THERAPIST: Okay, what would you like to be different about that?
>
> CLIENT: Well, I want to be able to go over there and not get so aggravated that I end up bingeing and really feeling bad about myself.

THERAPIST: That makes sense. I am curious, do you want to go over and not get aggravated or go over and not binge? (*Here we are looking to clarify the goal, which may also challenge the client's belief.*)

CLIENT: Wow. That is a good question.....I'm not sure. I think it is unrealistic to think that I won't ever get aggravated over there, because my family makes me nuts and I can't change who they are, as much as I'd like to. So, I guess what I'd like is to be in control enough that I wouldn't start bingeing in order to cope.

THERAPIST: That sounds reasonable. So what would need to happen for you to be in control enough?

CLIENT: It would have to start before we got there.

THERAPIST: How would you do that?

CLIENT: Well, I have tried to talk with my partner on the way over to my parents' house and come up with a way to be supported while we are there. I know my partner wants to, but once she gets in that environment she becomes like one of them and that upsets me even more.

THERAPIST: So has this strategy worked so far?

CLIENT: I guess I would have to say no, as much as I wish it could work.

THERAPIST: What else could you do to gain some control on the way over to your parents' house?

CLIENT: Well, I'm not sure, because my partner usually drives and they don't live very far away.

THERAPIST: So your partner usually drives? (*I repeated this to draw client's attention to the pattern.*)

CLIENT: Yes.

THERAPIST: What could you do differently before going to your parents' house that would make you feel in control?

CLIENT: Well, now that I am sitting here talking, it occurs to me that I wonder if it would help if I drove over. I always feel more in control when I am driving somewhere.

THERAPIST: Really. That's interesting. So you are saying that when you drive you feel more in control and so if you drive over to your parents ' house then you'll gain some control and ... what will be different for you?

CLIENT: Well, I'm guessing here (*this is a common qualifier*), but I think that if I can drive over and feel in charge then I will enter their house feeling more empowered, and it won't bother me as much when they start doing their thing.

THERAPIST: Okay. What else will be different for you?

CLIENT: If I can feel in control then I won't need to binge in order to gain some control and then I will really feel stronger when they all start picking on me. I think my partner will probably notice and maybe even come to my defense for a change...although I won't count on it.

THERAPIST: This sounds like an interesting solution to try. How confident are you that you can do this?

CLIENT: Oh, very. I don't think it will be a big deal for her to let me drive over.

In this example the client was able to shift her proposed solution from talking in the car ride over to driving there herself. This slight shift involved some insight on her part. We purposely did not make the suggestion that she drive over to her parents' house. Rather, we asked questions about the pattern and let her come to this solution. We find this to be a very challenging aspect of this model. Clinicians have often asked us if this model utilizes insight, and the answer is yes, depending on the client's needs. Some clients already have an enormous amount of insight and are stuck anyway, and other clients need to make a shift in their assumptions in order to make lasting changes. We find that when we challenge our clients' beliefs in order to shift them out of a box, this usually involves a certain amount of insight.

INTEGRATION ISSUES

Understanding your success. As you begin to think about your current clients and what relationship they have to each goal, you will understand why some tasks have worked and some have not.

Doing something different. When working with clients in the future or with current clients who are not reporting progress, this is a piece of the model that you can utilize to help you shift the client toward progress. We find these concepts most useful when we are feeling frustrated by a lack of client progress or when we find ourselves trying to convince our clients of something. These are both scenarios in which we review the "relationship" and typically find we have misunderstood something.

Working with multiple goals. When working with couples and families we find it helpful to break down each goal and each person's relationship to that goal. This helps clarify and simplify what may seem like a chaotic system.

The triad. It is important to remember that the client-therapist-problem relationship is goal specific. Later in the first session we change the triad to be the client-therapist-*goal* relationship. As illustrated by the above example of the client with the diagnosis of an eating disorder, she had different relationships with different goals.

The box. The schematic of *The Box* is not limited in use to the complainant-listener type relationship. Clients in the customer-seller type relationship can also be "in boxes," as the example below illustrates.

4

Creating Well-Formed Treatment Goals

The intention of Solution Focused Brief Therapy is for clients to reach *their* goals in a time-effective manner and for clients to drive the work. Before any goal can be achieved, it must first be clearly defined and "well formed" (Friedman & Fanger, 1991; Berg & Miller, 1992). When goals are well formed, both the client and the therapist will know when the goals have been reached, and therefore know when it is time to stop therapy. This is not to say that the therapist does not play any role in setting the goals. When we examine the process, it becomes clear to us that we have a large influence in how the goals are defined. We view goals as being co-created by the therapist and client in the first session. As Alice in Wonderland found out, if you do not know where you are going you are bound to end up somewhere; it just might not be where you wanted to go (Carroll, 1988).

Well-formed goals have many characteristics. The following is our conceptualization of well-formed goals.

Salient to the client

A goal must be important to, and within our clients' control Anyone who has worked with adolescents knows how challenging this can be. Oftentimes we have to work very hard to find a goal that is important to these clients, not just important to parents, teachers, or partners.

Smaller rather than larger

Setting too large a goal increases the chances that it will not be met, or if it is, no one will notice. Doing Solution Focused work becomes easier when we help our clients break down their goals.

> *CLIENT*: I really want to build my self-esteem.
> *THERAPIST*: What is going to be the first sign to you that you are beginning to build your self-esteem?
> *CLIENT*: When I get a job.
> *THERAPIST*: Okay, what is the first step to getting a job?
> *CLIENT*: Well, I guess I have to write my resume.
> *THERAPIST*: And what is the first step to writing your resume?
> *CLIENT*: I have to figure out what I need to include in the resume.
> *THERAPIST*: Where are you going to get that information?
> *CLIENT*: I think the library has some books on that.
> *THERAPIST*: Okay, what will it take for you to get to the library?
> *CLIENT*: I need to get my partner to watch the kids for an hour.

This may seem laborious; however, when you break the goal down this small it becomes easier for the client to achieve. This is also a process that we teach clients to do for themselves, so that they begin to integrate the ability to break down goals for themselves. This is often why clients tell us they want to terminate before their goals are completely achieved; it is because they know they can break it down and take it one small step at a time.

Realistic, doable, and achievable

It is very important that we negotiate realistic, doable, and achievable goals with our clients. When clients state that they want to work on winning the lottery, we will try to negotiate a more doable goal (unless of course they have a good method for winning). We have found that we must be cautious when determining what is realistic and doable for another person. The following case vignette illustrates this point.

Case Example: Jon was a 19-year-old referred to the clinic by his probation officer for breaking and entering. He had been expelled from two schools, the second for throwing a large desk at the principal. He had several run-ins with the law. Before Jon's arrival the probation officer sent over an inch-thick psychological profile that stated that Jon was diagnosed with a conduct disorder, and antisocial personality disorder.

> *THERAPIST*: So, what would you like to work on?
> *CLIENT*: I want to program computer games for Nintendo.
> *THERAPIST*: Wow, what makes you want to do that?
> *CLIENT*: Well, I play the games all day long, and so far I have beat every one of them.
> *THERAPIST*: Okay, what is the first step in reaching that goal?
> *CLIENT*: Getting a job with them, I guess.
> *THERAPIST*: Hm, considering you did not finish high school, are there other things you have to do first?
> *CLIENT*: Well, get my G.E.D., I guess; oh yeah, I would have to know how to program more than I do.
> *THERAPIST*: You already know how to program some?
> *CLIENT*: Sure. I took a course in school, got an A.

THERAPIST: Okay, what is the first step in getting a
G.E.D.?...

As it turns out, Jon did get his G.E.D. and went on to take some courses
at the local community college before we lost touch with him. When we
started working with Jon we had serious doubts about whether he would
ever (or should ever) program for Nintendo. However, by breaking down
the goals we were able to create with Jon some goals that were realistic,
doable, and achievable.

Start of something and the presence of something

It is much easier to begin working on a goal and to continue that
work when you are starting, instead of stopping, something. For example,
it is easier to start eating right than to lose weight, just as it's easier to
communicate in a calmer way than to stop yelling. For one thing it is
measurable. A goal is also easier to work on when it is the presence of
something, rather than the absence of something. It is the difference
between moving toward something as opposed to away from something.
For example, stopping drinking is the absence of drinking. Working on
sobriety is easier and more focused. When a client negotiates a goal that

is the absence of something and/or
stopping something, a vacuum can be
created. In addition, the brain does not
process the word *not* very well. If we
asked you now to close your eyes and
whatever you do, *do not imagine a big,
smelly, silly-looking elephant.* For most
people you must first imagine the elephant
and then cross it out, cover it up, erase it,
or do some other internal event to remove
it. In the same way, when clients are
trying to lead a sober life, it makes it
much more difficult if they are walking around saying to themselves, "I
can't drink, I can't go to the bar, I can't hang out with my friends who

drink." All they are thinking about is what they cannot do, instead of thinking about what they can do.

Concrete, specific, and behavioral

The more concrete, specific, and behavioral the goals are, the easier it is going to be for the client and the therapist to notice when they are achieved. The process of negotiating and reframing the goals to be more concrete, specific, and behavioral helps connect the client's different thoughts, beliefs, and feelings. For example:

> *THERAPIST*: So when you are happier, what else will be different?
> *CLIENT*: My aura will be a different color.
> *THERAPIST*: What color will it be?
> *CLIENT*: Red.
> *THERAPIST*: So when your aura is red, what will you be doing differently?
> *CLIENT*: You mean behaviorally?
> *THERAPIST*: Yes.
> *CLIENT*: Well, I'll be going for more walks, I'll have more energy, I'll...

It is important that we do not ignore the emotional content during the session. Many people who observe a Solution Focused session are confused by this process of operationalizing the client's feelings. Rather than ignoring them, we embrace them and work with the client to explore the feelings' impact on the client.

Interactional

No action operates completely in a vacuum. When clients make a change in their lives, it is noticed by others and effects others. The more we can define the goal in interactional terms the better. The following example comes from a session with a family involving a 14-year-old girl, her mother, and her father.

> CLIENT (*14-year-old*): I know what will solve this
> problem.
> THERAPIST: Okay, what?
> CLIENT: I need my own phone.

When we were first learning Solution Focused therapy we jumped on this bait. If we had known at the time about interactional questions, we would not have gone down the path we did. What we proceeded to do in this session was to ask all sorts of questions about the phone. Scott Miller (1992b) described this as "hostage negotiations" (what type of phone, what color, call waiting, etc.). What he suggested and what we did in the subsequent session was this:

> THERAPIST: So when you get this phone, what
> difference is this going to make with the
> problems that brought you here today?
> CLIENT: Well, when I get my own phone, Dad will get
> his phone messages, Dad and I will not get into
> fights, Mom won't have to defend me, they won't
> fight. We will all just get along better.
> THERAPIST: So when you get your own phone, you will
> all just get along better?
> CLIENT: Right.
> THERAPIST: What else will be different?
> CLIENT: I won't have to get angry when they ask me to
> get off the phone....

Contextual

It is important to know when and where clients want to achieve their goals. In our experience most goals do have a frame around them.

Case Example: An 18-year-old high school senior stated that he wanted to be more "normal." At first we assumed this meant all the time. It soon became apparent he wanted to be "normal" only some of the time.

THERAPIST: I'm confused. How much of the time do
you want to be normal?

CLIENT: Only 40%.

THERAPIST: So when you are being normal, what are
you doing differently?

CLIENT: Paying attention in class and not being the class clown.
Sometimes this can get me in trouble, but most of the
time, when I am not in class, it helps me be popular.

Measurable

Along with all the other components of well-formed goals, being
measurable is vital. When we can measure a goal, it is much easier to
follow progress, and determine what is working. We will talk further
about measuring goals in the section on scaling (see Chapter 8).

INTEGRATION ISSUES

Utilizing well-formed goals. Regardless of your treatment modality this
is a piece of the model that you can integrate into your practice. Thinking
about well-formed goals will help clarify many confusing cases.

Justifying treatment. In this era of managed care and demanding funding
sources it is important to be working with well-formed goals and to be
able to articulate these to the payor. This is a way for clinicians to bring a
concrete and quantitative assessment to the work we do, which is anything
but an exact science.

Clarifying whose goal it is. Oftentimes clinicians who work for larger
agencies find themselves being asked to impose agency agendas on their
clients. By breaking down each goal we can assess whether it is well
formed and quickly realize whose goal it is. We can assume that working

on a goal that is "salient to the client" will achieve success quicker than if the goal is not something in which the client is invested. This clarification has helped many clinicians working in protective services, probation, involuntary programs, state programs, and the medical arena.

.

5

Beginning the First Interview

There are a great many tasks that we want to accomplish during our first encounter with clients. Given the current requirements of insurance, particularly managed care plans, we must often make a clear diagnosis, articulate behavioral treatment goals, establish rapport, and begin treatment all in the first hour.

We focus on several goals during the first Solution Focused interview:

- Create a safe and therapeutic environment for the client
- Establish rapport with the client
- Begin to create treatment goals with the client

The primary tools for the interview are the questions that we pose to our clients. With this in mind, the nature of the questions we ask is intended to help move clients toward their solutions. Although it is not

necessary nor always appropriate to conduct a session in the sequence
below, we have found that most of the time, the first session flows in this
order. The determining factor is following the client and moving to the
next stage when the client is ready. Therefore we will present the
following order for now, and later talk about different variations based on
specific needs.

TREATMENT AND FEE AGREEMENT
WHAT BRINGS YOU HERE TODAY?
MIRACLE QUESTION
EXCEPTIONS
SCALING
HISTORY GATHERING (if necessary)
ANYTHING ELSE
CONSULTATION BREAK
INTERVENTION MESSAGE

Treatment and fee agreement

As the world of managed behavioral health care (mental health
and substance abuse) continues to expand, establishing clear boundaries
and clearly setting the stage for any therapeutic encounter have become
very important. Our treatment and fee agreement has expanded and
grown over the past few years as more information needs to be clearly
outlined for our clients. We spend approximately ten minutes at the
beginning of any session when there is a new person in the room reviewing
these forms and answering all of their questions. It no longer constitutes
informed consent to have our clients read and sign these forms in the
waiting room. It is important to check with your state licensing board,
your trade association, and we highly recommend your legal counsel, for
changes in the field that need to be reflected in these forms. During this
stage of the session we also explain to the client the team approach and
the break. This is how we typically state this:

We utilize a team approach in our work. This means that during the session, usually after 40 or 45 minutes, I will take a break and go consult with my clinical team. The team is bound by the same confidentiality rules that I am. If someone on the team knows you in anyway he or she will leave immediately at the beginning of the session . The team is made up of other people who work or train here. After the break I will come back and give you some feedback from the team. If there is no team available, I will still take a break, talk to the team in between sessions, and then integrate what we talk about into the next session. If there is not going to be a next session or there is a lot of time between sessions, I will either call you or write you a letter if the information cannot wait. We use the team because we have found that our clients reach their goals faster when we do.

And when we are using a two-way mirror we add:

Let me tell you about the mirror. This is a two-way mirror and we have a team of clinicians observing this session (*we have also told people about this when they call and in the literature they receive beforehand*). The team may buzz in on the phone like this (*phone rings*). When this happens it means that the team wants me to go in a different direction, or ask a particular question. It usually means they want me to do something different, not you.

What brings you here today?

There are many ways a clinician can begin the first session. This is another example of how assumptions drive the work that we do. We have heard many opening questions over the years, and a brief survey has created the following list:

What can I do for you today?
What is the problem?
How may I help you?
How may I help you with your problem?
What is it you would like to have happen here today?

Each of these opening questions has one or more assumptions driving it. For example, "How may I help you with your problem?" may have the following assumptions behind it:

1. There is a problem.
2. This person wants my help with this problem.
3. I can help this person with the problem.

        The first question we tend to ask in a Solution Focused interview is, *"What brings you here today?"* If we are doing a home visit we ask, *"What brings me here today?"* This question sets the tone of a Solution Focused interview from the start, and serves as an invitation to our clients to tell their story. The answer may often include how the client defines and thinks about the problem, how the problem originated and when, and who is involved in the problem. This may be a one-sentence answer, such as "My wife left me," or may take thirty minutes to answer. We ask each person in the room this opening question. The task of the therapist during this part of the interview is to *acknowledge* the client's story. Acknowledgment is defined as "recognition of someone's or something's existence, validity, authority, or right. An answer or response in return for something done (*The American Heritage Dictionary, Second College Edition, 1991*). This is distinguished from *amplifying* what the client tells you. To amplify means, "to make larger or more powerful; increase. To add to, as by illustrations; make complete. To exaggerate (*The American Heritage Dictionary, Second College Edition, 1991*). The quintessential amplification we learned in social work school, often quoted sarcastically, is, "Tell me more about your mother." It is important to stress that when therapists choose amplification as a technique, they are not poor clinicians. Our goal is to be aware of when we amplify and for what reason. At times we will choose to amplify, for not doing so would jeopardize rapport. Other times we may be just plain curious.

We make a conscious effort to acknowledge the clients' stories as much as possible, in an attempt to understand our clients' views of the world. We try to give the message that we have heard what clients are saying. A significant piece of this acknowledgment is empathy. Good clinicians are empathic, but this does not necessarily mean we need to amplify the problem. In this section of the session we want to acknowledge both verbally and nonverbally what clients tell us.

Verbally: We often will say those monosyllable statements that we were told in school never to say: Uh-huh, sure, of course, that's right. This lets clients know in an auditory way that we have heard them. It is important to use these in response to our clients, not randomly.

Nonverbally: It is also important to nonverbally acknowledge what clients say to us. We do this by nodding, writing down certain comments, making eye contact, and leaning forward. By writing something down we believe we are sending the message to our clients that what they are saying is important enough for us to be writing it down. Therefore, we are very aware that what we write down and highlight is important.

It is important to continue this phase of acknowledgment until clients give you an *invitation* to ask the next question. By an invitation we mean a signal from clients that they have completed telling us their story to the extent they feel is necessary at the present time and that we have adequately acknowledged this story. Typically clients will stop talking, look at us, and seem to say, "your turn, ask another question." It can take some practice and a little finesse to determine when you have heard enough and when the client has told you enough during this initial stage. For example:

> *THERAPIST*: What brings you here today?
> *CLIENT*: My mother made me come. *(Client stops talking, looks at the ground)*

If you assume that this is all your client needs or wants to say, he or she may bring this information up later in the interview. We consider this "problem talk" (deShazer, 1994) and prefer to limit it to the first part of the interview when we can. Particularly with mandated clients we have found it important to ask some amplifying questions to clarify why they are in our office. In this category of clients we include most adolescents, spouses, court and protective service clients, and anyone sent by someone else.

> THERAPIST: (*continued from above*) Do you have a
> sense of what your mother wanted to accomplish
> by having you come here today?
> CLIENT: She is probably going to say she wants me to
> stop using pot and go to school.

Oftentimes our clients, particularly those who are referred from other therapists, have an idea of what they should or need to tell us during the first session. It is not that these clients are "resistant" to a Solution Focused approach, but rather they are trying to cooperate with us. If you went to the same therapist for 15 visits and each time the first thing the therapist asked you was to describe how you were feeling that day, you would have every reason to expect that the next therapist would do the same thing. This trend has decreased over the past few years as more consumers of mental health services have become better educated about the differences in the field.   However, we do find that clients who have previously seen a therapist sometimes expect us to amplify more of the problem for them. With these clients we tend to make a conscious effort to acknowledge until the client feels understood. In some   cases our agencies expect us to gather history. Since this is not a focus of our treatment we clarify this discrepancy for our clients by saying that "at the end of our session we may need to ask you some questions for our agency forms, which may or may not have anything to do with treatment." Below is an example of how we explain gathering "problem-oriented" information to our clients.

THERAPIST: Now that we have gone over the treatment and fee, why don't we move on? For the rest of the hour we are going to talk, and right before I take my break, I may ask you some questions that have nothing to do with why you are here, but I have to fill out this form for the agency [*Note: We say this to clarify that such information as socioeconomic data, educational level, past therapy, hospitalizations, and other information is not necessarily relevant to the current treatment; however, we need the information as part of our intake process.*] Okay? Fine, why don't you tell me what brings you here today?

CLIENT: My mom thinks I have an eating disorder.

THERAPIST: What do you think?

CLIENT: Well, I think she is overreacting and all over my case.

THERAPIST: Okay, do you think she needs to be here to work this out?

CLIENT: Probably, because I don't think there's a problem.

At this juncture we would invite the mother in to join us. We are making the client the expert about who needs to be in treatment to solve this problem. This is based on the assumption that clients have the resources and strengths to solve their complaints. The client now feels in control and empowered. We are also agreeing with the client's view of the world.

INTEGRATION ISSUES

Rejecting the team approach. Many clinicians ask us if clients have a difficult time with the team approach. We have had very few clients over the years who have refused a live team. A partial explanation for this is the fact that we tell clients on the phone during our intake process that we use the team, and some (although the numbers are very low) decide to go elsewhere for services. When we are using a team we can sometimes tell when a client is uncomfortable with the team watching. The client will ask a lot of questions about the team, how many members there are, and on rare occasions ask to meet the team. When this is the case the team is careful not to phone in too often.

You mean I don't have to tell my story again? During the beginning of the first session clients will sometimes ask how much of their story they need to tell. We respond by saying, "You only need to tell me as much as you feel I need to know right now to get us started." Clients are often relieved that they do not need to tell their whole story for the twelfth time. When clients are not sure how much of the story is enough, we ask them to give us the condensed version, and assure them we will ask for more information if we need it.

Clients who only talk about the problem. In some cases (often people who have been in long term treatment before), clients begin to tell their story and no matter how much you acknowledge their story they keep talking about the problem. We continue to acknowledge their pain, their endurance, while periodically attempting to shift them towards talking about what they want to be different. In some cases clients are able to make this shift; however, when clients need to talk about their problem for the entire first session we follow their need. It is always important to figure out what clients want or need from treatment and try to provide that for them.

6

The Miracle Question

Once we feel rapport has been established with each person in the room and we have heard each story, it is then time to move on to the Miracle Question. By far the most famous of the Solution Focused questions, a great deal has been written about the Miracle Question (Berg & Miller, 1992; deShazer, 1988, 1994; Dolan, 1991; Friedman & Fanger, 1991). The Miracle Question is a future-based question with hypnotic qualities. By this we mean that it directs clients toward the future. The question is intended as a beginning, a way to create a picture or sense of what clients want. It is not, however, intended as the definition of the entire therapeutic episode. The Miracle Question should be said slowly while matching each client's pace. There are two ways we readily assess a client's pace. The first is to listen to the rhythm of speech. Some people talk very quickly, others talk slowly. The other technique we use is to notice the client's breathing, which works well to identify a client's internal pace. The Miracle Question goes as follows:

>*Suppose* tonight, after our session, you go
>home, and fall asleep, and while you are sleeping a
>miracle happens. The miracle is that **the problems that
>brought you here today** are solved! But you don't know
>that the miracle has happened because you are asleep.
>When you wake up in the morning, what will be some of
>the first things you will **notice** that will be different to
>tell you this miracle has happened?

The boldfaced sections are those that we feel are important not to change.
Suppose invites the client to pretend that this miracle has happened. It is
important not to say, "If tonight..." We make the presupposition that this
miracle is going to happen, and in fact already has. We also use the word
"when" as much as possible throughout our sessions. **The problems that
brought you here today** focuses the question. If instead you say, "Your
problems are solved," the answers you get tend from our experience to be
more grandiose (I'll win the lottery, have a bigger house, etc.). The third
important piece is "**notice,**" which encompasses all visual, auditory, and
kinesthetic responses.

After asking the Miracle Question it is important to:

- Wait for the client to respond; this may take some time.
- Ask each person in the room (we typically begin with the youngest
  person in the room).
- Remind clients that this is their miracle (not their mother's, partner's).

Many clients have never thought about what life will be like when their
problem is solved. At times clients cry after pondering this question for a
minute. Susan once had a client, the wife in a session with a couple, go
into such a trance that she did not begin to respond for four minutes!

Often, particularly with adolescents, they will first respond with,
"I don't know." Don't panic! This is very normal and, for some, a kind
of knee-jerk reaction to an unusual question. We will often tell clients to
take their time and really think about it. Another typical response from
children and adolescents is that they nod and say yes throughout the time

you are asking the Miracle Question and then blankly stare at you when you are done, and ask, "What was the question?" Adolescents are so used to "yessing" adults that you may need to repeat the question. When you are dealing with a couple, family, group, or some other combination, it is important to ask each person, even a young child, to respond to the Miracle Question. We have found that children as young as six-years-old can answer this question when asked in the format above. For younger children than that we will rephrase the question using wishes, a magic wand, or a magic lamp. Jordan had a young (and bright) girl ask him if she had a lamp could she ask for more than three wishes or was she limited to three like Aladdin!

We will often clearly delineate each client's response:

> *THERAPIST*: Okay Mom, that was your son's miracle, your miracle may be very different. So, what would you notice that is different?

There are also several follow-up questions to the Miracle Question that help to expand the answer to create a clear, broad picture of what the person's life is going to be like after the miracle happens and the problems are solved.

One of the profound effects of the Miracle Question is to shift the client's focus away from the "how" (a miracle) to the "what" as illustrated below (for further details see section on The Box, Chapter 3):

How am I going to solve this problem?

What will be different (in my life, marriage, job)
when this problem is solved?

Some of the typical questions we ask in a first session are illustrated below in bold type.

THERAPIST: So, **what brings you here today**?

CLIENT: Well, as I mentioned to you on the phone, I have a history of panic attacks. I have had them for the past nine years, off and on. During the past two years they have really been under control.

THERAPIST: Okay.

CLIENT: In the past month I have had three close relatives die, and I am beginning to see some of the warning signs that the attacks are coming back.

THERAPIST: Okay, are you currently taking any medication?

CLIENT: My doctor prescribes a beta-blocker.

THERAPIST: Okay. Is there anything else that is bringing you here today?

CLIENT: I had a daughter 10 months ago, and I am concerned about my parenting. My mother is driving me nuts and making me question my competence as a mother. I really want to deal differently with my mom (*client cries*).

THERAPIST: Take your time.

CLIENT: In the past, counseling has been helpful.

THERAPIST: **What was helpful about it?**

CLIENT: I always find it helpful to talk to someone about what is going on.

THERAPIST: Okay, that makes sense. I am going to ask you an unusual question. **Suppose tonight, after our session, you go home and fall asleep, and while you are sleeping a miracle happens. The miracle is that the problems that brought you here today are solved! But you don't know that the miracle has happened because you were asleep. When you wake up in the morning, what will be some of the first things**

you will notice that will be different to tell you this miracle has happened?

CLIENT: Wow, I have no idea!

THERAPIST: Well, think about it for a second.

CLIENT: I'd know that I was a good mother!

THERAPIST: Okay, **what else will you notice?**

CLIENT: My mother would keep her mouth shut.

THERAPIST: Okay, you will know you are a good mother, your mother will keep her mouth shut (*repeating*); **what else will be different**?

CLIENT: I will not feel like I am the only one on the planet that has panic attacks. I mean I know on an intellectual level that other people have this, but sometimes I feel really alone.

THERAPIST: **So when this miracle happens, what will be different about that?**

CLIENT: Well, I guess I might be talking to other people that have panic attacks, and just not feel this way.

THERAPIST: **How will you feel instead?**

CLIENT: Okay about having panic attacks. Well, if it were a true miracle, I would not have them.

THERAPIST: That's right. **And when you are not** having the panic attacks**, what else will be different in your life?**

CLIENT: Well, my self-esteem will be higher.

THERAPIST: **And when your** self-esteem **is** higher, **what will be different**?

It is important to remember that each new question is based on the client's last response. Clients report to us that they feel in control of the pace and how "deep" they go in a session. The next example illustrates other questions we ask clients as follow-up to the miracle question.

Case Example: An adolescent girl comes in with her mother.

> *THERAPIST*: **So what brings you here today?**
> *CLIENT*: Well, I am overweight (*client starts crying*)...
> and I need to get under control.
> *THERAPIST*: Okay, is there anything else?
> *CLIENT*: No, except that I've been like this ever since I
> can remember but now I'm in 10th grade and I
> know that the boys won't date me if I'm this fat
> and I'd have more friends if I was thinner.
> *THERAPIST*: Okay, that makes sense. Let me ask you
> an unusual question. **Suppose tonight, after our
> session, you go home and fall asleep, and while
> you are sleeping a miracle happens. The
> miracle is that the problems that brought you
> here today are solved! But you don't know
> that the miracle has happened because you
> were asleep. When you wake up in the
> morning, what will be some of the first things
> you will notice that will be different to tell you
> this miracle has happened?**
> *CLIENT:* Wow – well, if it was a miracle I would feel
> better about myself. I would be happier, look
> better, get attention from guys, have more
> friends.
> *THERAPIST:* **Right. And when you are feeling better
> about yourself what else will be different?**
> *CLIENT:* Well, I'll be more confident and not so shy.
> I'll have more friends and go on dates and feel
> like a popular girl for the first time. (*We pursued
> this further and obtained many more details
> about how she would be different and how this
> would affect her relationships with other
> people.*)

THERAPIST: **Of course; and who would be the first person to notice this miracle had happened?**

CLIENT: My family.

THERAPIST: **What would your family notice?**

CLIENT: They will notice that I'm happier, that I look different, thinner. My family will be happier and I'll have more of a social life and go out.

THERAPIST: **When your family is happier, what difference will it make?**

CLIENT: I'm not sure. I think they will be more relaxed and enjoy each other's company more. Mom and Dad will probably spend more time together and not worry about me as much.

THERAPIST: **That makes sense. So who will be the next to notice?**

CLIENT: My friends will notice that I am in a daze, doing better in school and more interested in studying and doing my homework, so then my grades will go up. (*This section of the session continued with the mom and client for about 25 minutes.*)

Some therapists are uncomfortable asking about a miracle. If you feel this is hokey or are uncomfortable, we encourage you to utilize the alternative future-based question below. Otherwise the question may be perceived as disingenuous. We have found that clinicians hesitate to ask the Miracle Question most often when certain events have recently occurred in a client's life or the client presents with a particular diagnosis or symptom. For example, with clients who have recently lost a spouse or child, or clients who have been diagnosed with a chronic or fatal disease, or live with chronic pain, we sometimes hesitate to ask about a miracle because we do not want the client to say to us, "My child would be alive again." Other clients (although this is rare) get stuck on or do not like the Miracle Question. For some this is due to not being able to get beyond the concept of a miracle happening to them, usually for religious reasons. In addition, very concrete or "logical" thinkers, such as male engineers, at times have difficulty imagining a miracle. When this occurs the following alternative question works almost as well:

> **Imagine** this is our last session and the **problems that brought you here today** are solved. What will you be **noticing** that is different to let you know that we do not need to meet anymore?

Notice that this version has the same key elements in bold print as you find with the Miracle Question. We have found in most cases that you can ask the Miracle Question, even if a person has experienced a recent loss. On occasion you will get the client who says, "My child [partner, parent] would be alive," or "I wouldn't have cancer." At times we are amazed when they do not say this! However, when they do we typically respond:

> CLIENT: Well, my partner would still be alive and I would not be HIV positive.
>
> THERAPIST: Of course (*long pause, being respectful of their loss and pain*). And what else would be different?

This accomplishes a subtle yet important goal; it lets the client know that this is a normal and often healthy desire.

Do not be too concerned about all of the variations on the questions that follow up the Miracle Question; with time and practice they will flow very naturally. As a summary, here are a few of the more common questions.

- *What else will be different when this miracle happens?*
- *So when you are happier [more in control, your husband is drinking less], what else will be different?* (Note the use of the word *when* and not *if*).
- *Who will be the first person to notice that this miracle has happened?*

- *What will he/she notice different about you?*
- *What will you notice different about him/her?*
- *When you do that and he does this, what difference will it make in your relationship?* (This gives the interactional aspect of their goal).

Although it is rare, there are times when a client cannot answer the Miracle Question. The vast majority of the time this is a strong diagnostic indicator for us. When a client cannot even begin to imagine what the future will be like when this problem is solved, this may mean the client has very little hope, may be suicidal (clearly worth asking about), and will need a tremendous amount of validation and support.

Other issues: You may have noticed that many of the questions are stated in the positive frame. Unfortunately, not all clients present their story in a positively framed way. There are some techniques we use to help clients begin to frame answers in a manner that addresses what they want, rather than what they do not want (the presence of something, instead of the absence of something). Below is an example:

> *THERAPIST: (Miracle Question)...So what will you notice that is different?*
>
> *CLIENT:* Well, I won't be doing drugs anymore.
>
> *THERAPIST:* Okay, what else?
>
> *CLIENT:* I won't be getting to work late?
>
> *THERAPIST:* **So when you are not doing drugs and not getting to work late, what will be different about those situations?** (*At times this question alone is enough to help the client begin to state goals in the positive.*)
>
> *CLIENT:* I won't feel as down all the time.
>
> *THERAPIST:* **How will you feel instead?**
>
> *CLIENT:* I guess I would have more energy and feel like doing something now and then.
>
> *THERAPIST:* So when you have more energy, what would you do?

CLIENT: Not get into so much trouble.

THERAPIST: **So when you are not doing drugs, and not getting into so much trouble, what else is not happening?** (*Note: For further information on the use of this double negative question, see Gallagher, 1992*)

CLIENT: I won't be stealing from my friends.

THERAPIST: What else won't you be doing?

CLIENT: I'd be taking more responsibility for myself.

When a client answers the Miracle Question by stating that other people will be doing things differently (complainant-listener type relationship), this is an indication that we need to follow the client. For example:

THERAPIST: So when this miracle happens, what will be different?

CLIENT: Well, my kids will be doing what they are supposed to.

THERAPIST: What will you notice them doing differently?

CLIENT: Well, they will get up in the morning, and get ready for school.

THERAPIST: And?

CLIENT: And won't be fighting with each other like they do all the time.

THERAPIST: So when they are doing these things, what else will be different?

CLIENT: The house will be quieter.

Once we have followed the client's lead with regard to who is changing, we can subtly change directions.

THERAPIST: So when your kids are doing all of those things, what do you think they are going to notice different about you?

CLIENT: Oh – that's easy, I won't be yelling so much.
THERAPIST: What else?
CLIENT: The oldest would say I would be "off his back."
THERAPIST: So when you are not yelling as much and off his back, what else will they notice different about you?
CLIENT: I'll be happier.

Once the client begins to talk in the first person we can begin to utilize the types of questions outlined above. In the above example the client was able to move rapidly to discussing goals. Another factor is to continually inquire about what a client means by particular words. We are often making assumptions about the meaning of happy, depressed, better, doing what they are told, and so on. Clarifying these common words adds depth to the clinical picture and our understanding of the client's goals.

INTEGRATION ISSUES

Using interactional questions. When we are working with more than one person, it is important to make our questions interactional. When we ask interactional questions, our clients start to figure out ways that their goals are related to each other. For example:

THERAPIST: What else will be different?
CLIENT1: He will talk more.
THERAPIST: So when he is talking more, what will he notice different about you?
CLIENT1: I won't be nagging him so much to talk to me.
THERAPIST: So when she is not nagging so much, what else will be different?
CLIENT2: We won't fight as often and I won't leave the house as much.

> *THERAPIST*: So when you are not leaving the house as
> much, what is different about your relationship?

We also ask clients we see in individual therapy interactional questions for similar reasons. This technique figuratively brings important people in the client's life into the treatment room.

Maintaining rapport. When we first started doing this type of work we received some excellent advice that we gladly pass on. No matter what type of questions you use in your work, do not lose sight of rapport. Given that Solution Focused therapy has a limited number of types of questions, we believe that it is easy to form a habit we call "machine-gunning" your client. By this we mean asking too many questions too rapidly. The hard part of doing Solution Focused work is having to wait for the client to respond to one question, before we can formulate and then ask the next. We want to be listening for what question the client just answered in case it was not what we thought we asked. This will indicate that we need to shift our questions to follow the client more closely.

Needing more information. At some point it may appear that the client has run out of things that will be different. If you feel more clarification is needed or the miracle is not broad enough, you can use the following technique.

> *THERAPIST*: So what else will be different when this
> miracle happens?
> *CLIENT*: My parents will know that I am telling the
> truth.
> *THERAPIST*: What will they see you doing to let them
> know that you are telling them the truth?
> *CLIENT*: Looking them in the eye when I talk.
> *THERAPIST*: What do you mean?
> *CLIENT*: When I am lying, I can't look in their eyes.
> *THERAPIST*: And what else would be different?
> *CLIENT*: That's it.

> THERAPIST: **Okay, so you will be happier, telling them the truth, looking them in the eye. And when you are doing those things, what else will be different?**

Ending the Miracle Question. At some point you will want to end this section of the session. In some cases the client may run out of things that will be different:

> THERAPIST: So what else will be different when this miracle happens?
> CLIENT: Nothing, that's all.

Or you may need to end it (usually due to time constraints). We do this by saying:

> THERAPIST: **Is there anything else** that will be different when this miracle happens?

By using the words, "is there" instead of "what else" we are offering the client the opportunity to say no or to add one more thing.

Reinforcing the miracle. We have found it helpful to incorporate a technique we learned from Dr. Scott Miller during this phase of the session. Scott will often repeat what the client has said will be different in order to reinforce the material. Keep in mind that this may be the first time the client has articulated these particular thoughts, and anything we can do to reinforce them will help the client retain the material.

> THERAPIST: So what else will be different when this miracle happens?
> CLIENT: I will be talking to my kids more and getting to work on time.
> THERAPIST: Okay, you will be talking to your kids more, getting to work on time; what else?

Another way to reinforce the client's answer is to make the client repeat the answer.

CLIENT: I will be talking to my kids more, getting to work on time, and and not yelling at my friends as much.
THERAPIST: Yes. So you would be talking to your kids more, getting to work on time, and what was the last one?
CLIENT: Not yelling at my friends as much.

Using interpretations. During our professional training most of us have become highly skilled in making connections for our clients and offering interpretations of the material they are presenting. We have found that these interpretations, although they may be very interesting, most often get in the way of clients' progress toward their goals. We therefore resist the urge to make the connections for our clients. This goes back to the assumption we discussed earlier that there is no one right way to view the world. We do, however, help our clients to make their own connections and give meaning to the events in their lives (insight).

Utilizing the client's language. In order to maintain rapport, we have found it very useful to subtly adopt the client's language when discussing the goals. For example, when a client refers to depression as feeling blue, the next time we refer to this we would use the client's expression of feeling blue.

Organizing the miracle response. Knowing where to go next in the Miracle Question part of the session is a common problem. Many people describe the response as an unorganized mish-mash of wishes. We have found several techniques useful in making sense of the responses we get to the Miracle Question. We will discuss three of these.

Horizontal responses: Some clients, when they begin to answer the Miracle Question, will introduce large categories. For example, they may say, "I will be..."

Happier	Enjoy work more	Get along better with my kids	Just feel better

When a client responds in this manner we continue by asking:

> *THERAPIST*: Okay, so you would be happier, enjoy work more, be getting along better with your kids, just feel better. What else?
>
> *CLIENT*: My wife and I would probably be getting along better also.
>
> *THERAPIST*: Okay, what else would be different?
>
> *CLIENT*: That's it.
>
> *THERAPIST*: Okay, let me go back to the first one. When you are feeling happier, what else will different?

Vertical responses: Some clients, when they begin to answer the Miracle Question, will introduce one category, and immediately begin to expand upon it: For example they may say, "I will be..."

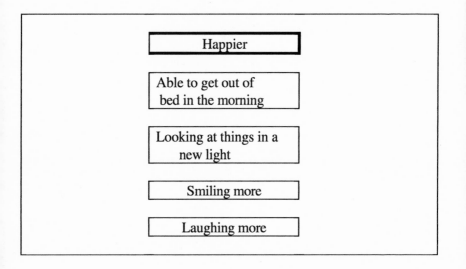

When clients respond in this manner we again follow their lead.

> *THERAPIST*: Okay, so you will be happier, and you will know this because you will be able to get out of bed, you will be smiling more, laughing more; what else will be different to let you know you are happier?
> *CLIENT*: I'd be talking more.
> *THERAPIST*: Okay, what else?
> *CLIENT*: That's it.

When the client has exhausted this topic, we will move on to the next.

THERAPIST: So when this miracle happens, you will be
   happier. What else will be different?
CLIENT: I will be enjoying work more.

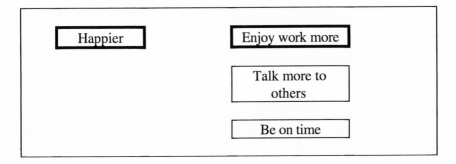

Mind mapping. The other technique we use is similar to the one
described above. When we believe that a client has stated a "big" topic,
we indicate this in our notes, and map the subcomponents of each large
item (Jensen, 1988).

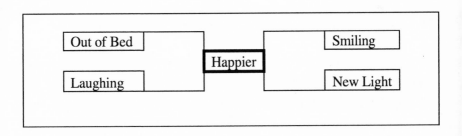

It's just a start. It is important to remember that the answer to the
Miracle Question is just where you and your client are going to start
treatment. It does not mean that all the things our clients mention in their
response to the Miracle Question will become well-formed goals, or be

worked on in treatment. We also do not assume that there is a particular order to the goals that they articulate. During the course of the session we may ask the client to prioritize these goals (see Scaling, Chapter 8).

Probing deeper.   You may feel that you are getting only superficial answers and not getting to the "deeper" issues.   One technique to get deeper is to back up and ask clients to explain something they just said.

CLIENT: When I'm less anxious I'll go out more with friends.
THERAPIST: Of course, and when you are going out more with friends what else is different?
CLIENT: I'll be more confident, happier, probably have more fun, feel like people want to be with me.
THERAPIST: **So when the miracle happens and you are going out more, what's changed that has made it possible for you to go out more?**
CLIENT: Huh! I'm not sure. I guess I would be feeling better about myself and would take the risk of asking someone out.

Exercise.   Try asking a colleague the Miracle Question.   Start off by asking your colleague to role play a cooperative client (you may need to remind her what a cooperative client says).   Practice asking the follow-up questions and mapping the responses.   You will become more comfortable with the pace and the type of questions each time to practice.

7

Exploring Exceptions

During the course of the interview clients will often mention times when the problem does not occur or is a little less severe. For example, we often hear:

I wish my kid would go to school more like he did today.
I want to feel less depressed, like I was last year.
I just wish he would treat me kinder, like it was my birthday all the time.
It was hard but I resisted the urge to drink yesterday.

These are exceptions (Berg & Miller, 1992) to the rule, and we want to expand upon these exceptions as much as possible. We think of exceptions as patterns of success (rather than failure). Clients will sometimes offer spontaneous exceptions during the miracle. After we have finished with the miracle we ask the following questions:

- *You mentioned you felt a little better on Tuesday.   What was different about Tuesday?*
- *You mentioned that your husband did not drink this past weekend. How do you explain that?*

If the client does not provide you with these spontaneous exceptions, we actively ask about those times that the problem is not a problem once we have a rich picture of the client's miracle (goals):

- *Tell me about times when small pieces of the miracle are happening already. What is different about those times?*
- *Tell me about those times when the problem does **not** happen?*
- *Many times people notice in between the time they make the appointment for therapy and the first session that things start to improve. What have you noticed about your situation?* (Weiner-Davis, deShazer, & Gingerish, 1987)

When we ask questions about exceptions, clients begin to notice more exceptions. For a multitude of reasons we have all been trained to look for what is not working, analyze it, write books about it, and study it until we completely understand how it does not work! Working with clients to identify what is working and then building upon these successes appears to be just as productive, if not more.

Case Example: Tammy is a 10-year-old girl referred due to "insomnia."

> *THERAPIST*: So, let me get this straight, you said that every now and then you do sleep through the night?
> *CLIENT*: Yep!
> *THERAPIST*: About how often does that happen?
> *CLIENT*: At least once a week.
> *THERAPIST*: So every week you are already sleeping through the night one time?
> *CLIENT*: Yep.
> *THERAPIST*: How do you do that?

CLIENT: I don't know. I have tried to think about it, but
I don't know how it happens.

Random versus deliberate exceptions

The preceding dialogue is an example of a random exception. In this case Tammy takes no responsibility for sleeping through the night, nor does she have any idea how it happens. The information is still very helpful and will be utilized when we develop a task for Tammy to do between sessions. We think of random exceptions as those that appear to be acts with no explanation. The client takes no responsibility for the exception occurring. There are times, however, when we ask clients to take a closer look at these random exceptions to learn more about them. Sometimes clients are able to realize that they have been responsible for the exceptions.

Deliberate exceptions, as the name implies, are those times when clients do something that creates the exception, and they can make the connection between their actions and the exception. For example:

THERAPIST: So when are those times now that you do
not drink?

CLIENT: Well, every now and then I go straight home
from work.

THERAPIST: So when you go straight home from work
you do not drink.

CLIENT: That's correct. In order for me to get to the bar
I have to make several turns off my route home.
The bar I go to is out of the way.

THERAPIST: And how do you end up going straight
home?

CLIENT: I just go home.

THERAPIST: Do you think about it at all or do you just
end up at home?

CLIENT: Oh, I think about it a lot. I usually sit in my
car for several minutes when I get out of work

> and wrestle with myself. Should I go home or to
> the bar?
> *THERAPIST*: So when home wins, how do you do that
> (notice the therapist chooses to amplify the
> exceptions, not the failure)?
> *CLIENT*: I just get tough with myself.

We sometimes help our clients to realize that they are indeed playing an active role in the creation of these exceptions by *positively blaming* (Berg & Miller, 1992; Miller, 1993b) them.

> *THERAPIST*: So when are those times that pieces of this
> miracle are already happening?
> *CLIENT*: Well, the other day I did feel a little better.
> *THERAPIST*: What was going on?
> *CLIENT*: Well, I went for a walk, and during the walk
> and for about an hour after I felt better.
> *THERAPIST*: **How did you know to take a walk?**
> *CLIENT*: Well, it just seemed like a good idea.
> *THERAPIST*: It was.

This helps to connect the actions our clients take with their feelings and their thoughts. It does not matter where clients enter the loop, whether they are motivated to take a walk and then feel better, or feel better so they take a walk. Either way clients are associating walking with feeling better.

Keep in mind that clients may not be able to identify any exceptions to their problems. This does not mean that all hope is lost and you should transfer this client to your first available colleague. The availability of exceptions is only one tool. By asking about exceptions we impose the assumption that no problem remains the same over time. Oftentimes by just asking about them in the first session clients will begin to notice them before the next session. In some cases some clients do have exceptions but they are so remote that they may not be useful to the work at hand. For example, a client that has not had a sober day in fifteen years may not fully recall what being sober is all about. We would still explore these exceptions for patterns of success that could be useful to the client today; however, we find most of the time these distant exceptions are not helpful.

INTEGRATION ISSUES

Getting comfortable with the questions. Most clinicians understand the concept of exceptions, but either gloss over them in a session or struggle with the structure of exception type questions. We found it helpful, initially, to have a page of sample exception questions that we could take into a session for referencing if we needed it.

Flexibility within the model. There are times when a client begins a first session by saying, "I'm not sure I need to be here anymore because things have turned around since I made the appointment:" When we hear something like this we tend to skip the Miracle Question and begin asking about exceptions.

Ask someone else. We almost always ask other people in the system if they have noticed any exceptions. You can get creative about who you ask. On an inpatient unit you can ask other patients in a group setting. In family therapy you can ask family members about what they notice about other family members. You can call people (probation officers, teachers) on the phone during a session, especially when you are sitting with mandated clients. One worker who does mostly home based work suggested that the worker may notice change that the client isn't able or ready to notice.

Clients who return to us. We also utilize exceptions when a client returns for another treatment episode. We view this as an opportunity to empower our clients and send the message that they must have been doing some things right in between treatment episodes.

Practicing on yourself. You can try an exercise of thinking about a problem you have and your own exceptions. Notice how it feels to elicit and amplify these exceptions. This will give you an idea of how powerful exceptions can be for our clients. This is certainly a piece of the model that can be integrated into any other treatment modality or protocol.

Another exercise is, at the end of the day, make yourself think about everything you did well during the day instead of all the mistakes you made. Another challenge is at staff meetings to encourage colleagues to talk about what they are doing that is working so we can all learn from each other. You will quickly realize that this paradigm shift is perhaps unnatural and profoundly powerful. If we cannot do this for ourselves, how can we know the right questions to ask our clients to elicit their exceptions?

8

Utilizing Scaling Questions

Scaling questions (Berg & Miller, 1992; deShazer, 1994) ask the client to rate themselves on a scale. We typically use a one-to-ten scale.

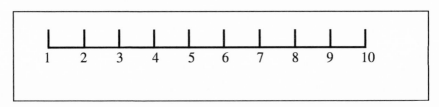

In the first session we use scaling to accomplish several tasks:

- Prioritize goals
- Set the next small step in treatment
- Evaluate willingness to change
- Evaluate confidence that change will occur

- Establish tools to measure specific goals that the client deems important

It is important to ask each participant in the session the scaling questions. During the first session we ask three different scaling questions.

Progress scaling question

The progress scale is used to determine where clients believe they are on a one-to-ten scale with reference to solving the problems that brought them to counseling. The progress scale also helps to determine the next small step toward clients' goals.

- *On a scale from 1 to 10, where 1 is when the problems that brought you here were at their worst and a 10 being when they are solved enough that you do not need to be here anymore, where would you say you are right now?*

When there is more than one person in the room we typically start with the youngest, and move up in age. One of our colleagues will sometimes have couples write their answers down and then show them to her so that the couple will not influence each other's answers. There are times when clients have difficulty quantifying their feelings, progress, or overall state of being. We must be patient and allow clients enough time to struggle with the idea of scaling progress. Very rapidly clients, groups, and systems become enamored with scaling questions. One ten-year-old boy came in for his second session declaring "I'm an eight!" It took Jordan a few minutes to figure out what he was referring to. The boy's mother stated, "He has been talking about this all week, rating himself everyday." This can become a self-monitoring tool for clients.

The next step question

The progress scaling question has a second part, and we call this the next step question. Again, we ask everyone in the room this question. The next step question can take one of two forms, active or passive. You may need to ask either active or passive for each client in the room. This should reflect their relationship to the goal (customer, complainant, visitor).

Active: If we believe that the client is going to take an active role in the next step, then we ask the scaling question in an active way. Typically these clients are in the customer-seller type relationship for that goal, meaning the client will do something to take responsibility for change.

* *If you are at a 3 now, what do you think you need to do to move you to a 3.5 or a 4?*

> THERAPIST: Okay, let me ask you another type of question. We will do this toward the end of each session. On a scale from 1 to 10, where 1 is when the problems that brought you here were at their worst and a 10 being when they are solved enough that you do not need to be here anymore, where would you say you are right now?
>
> CLIENT: Hm, one's the worst?
>
> THERAPIST: Correct.
>
> CLIENT: I'd say I'm about a 3.
>
> THERAPIST: Okay, so if you are a 3 right now, what do you need to do so that the next time we meet you can say you are a 3.5?
>
> CLIENT: Maybe go to school one more day this week.

Passive: If you believe that the client is not going to take an active role in the next step, but rather is going to be looking for someone or something else to make a small change, then it is more effective to ask the next step question in the passive manner. These clients are typically in the complainant-listener or visitor-host type relationships for that goal, in which case we will probably use this passive version of the next step scale.

- *If you are at a 3 now, what needs to happen for you to be able to say you are at a 3.5 or 4?*

> CLIENT: I'd say I'm about a 3.
>
> THERAPIST: Okay, so if you are a 3 right now, what needs to happen for you to be able to say you are at a 3.5?
>
> CLIENT: My kids would need to go to school one more day this week.

Sometimes the next step that the client gives is not a small step at all; rather, it is very large. Other times it may be difficult to determine whether the next step is a realistic one, or a leap across a large abyss. We will often ask our clients to break the next step down into very small pieces until we reach a point that both client and therapist believe the next step will happen readily, before the next session if there is going to be one.

> CLIENT: I'd say I'm about a 3.
>
> THERAPIST: Okay, so if you are a 3 right now, what do you need to do so that you can say you are a 3.5?
>
> CLIENT: Maybe go to school one more day this week.
>
> THERAPIST: Okay, and what would be the first step in getting yourself to school one more day this week?
>
> CLIENT: I'd have to get up in the morning, and go.
>
> THERAPIST: What do need to do to get up and go in the morning?
>
> CLIENT: Set my alarm and go to bed before 2:00 a.m.
>
> THERAPIST: Okay, so there are two steps there, go to bed earlier and set your alarm.
>
> CLIENT: Yeah.
>
> THERAPIST: What will it take for you to do that?
>
> CLIENT: Well, I've already started going to bed earlier; I guess I could write myself a note to set the alarm and ask my mother to check it before she goes to bed. (*Note the exception here.*)

> THERAPIST: And how likely is that to happen?
> CLIENT: I think there is a good chance.

There are times that the client's next step is not that obvious, and we have to ask several additional questions to clarify the step.

> THERAPIST: Okay, let me ask you another type of question. We will do this toward the end of each session. On a scale from 1 to 10, where 1 is when the problems that brought you here were at their worst and a 10 being when they are solved enough that you do not need to be here anymore, where would you say you are right now?
> CLIENT: Maybe a 2.
> THERAPIST: Okay, so if you are a 2 now, what will you have to do to get yourself to a 2.5? (*Notice this is the active version.*)
> CLIENT: I'm not sure. I guess I would just feel a little better.
> THERAPIST: So when you are feeling just a little better, that would be enough to bring you up to a 2.5?
> CLIENT: I think so.
> THERAPIST: Okay, so when you are feeling a little better, what are going to be the signs to you that this is occurring?
> CLIENT: What do you mean?
> THERAPIST: Well, when you are feeling better, what will you do differently?
> CLIENT: I might smile more.
> THERAPIST: Great, that's a good way to tell. So when you are smiling more that is a clear sign that you are feeling better.
> CLIENT: Yes.
> THERAPIST: What else will be a small sign to you that you are feeling just a little better?

CLIENT: I might sit with someone else at lunch and talk
to them.
THERAPIST: Good, that is also a clear sign.

It is very important that we deal with the emotional aspects of our
clients' lives. By asking the types of questions in the above example, we
are beginning to heighten our client's awareness that his thoughts and
feelings are connected.

Willingness scaling question

This scaling question measures the client's willingness to work on
solving the presenting problems. Again, it is important to ask each person
in the session. If by this point in the session you have not been able to
determine the relationship among the client, therapist, and goal, the
answer to this question can help to clarify the relationship. When clients
are in the customer-seller type relationship with a goal they are usually at
least a five on this scale. If clients report being lower than a five, it may
indicate they are in the complainant-listener type relationship.

• *On a scale from 1 to 10, where 1 is that you are not really willing to
work on solving these problems, and 10 is that you will do almost
anything to solve these problems (or achieve these goals), how
willing are you?*

The answer to the willingness question can be very telling. Regardless of
the answer we do not ask a next step question here. When dealing with
couples, families, and adolescents, the answer can provide valuable
information for us and the other people in the session.

THERAPIST: On a scale from 1 to 10, where 1 is that
you are not really willing to work on solving
these problems, and 10 is that you will do almost
anything to solve them, how willing are you?
MOTHER: 3.
DAUGHTER: 8.5.

THERAPIST: (*To daughter*) I'm curious why your answer is so much higher than your mother's.

DAUGHTER: Ask her.

MOTHER: I'm not really willing to work on this anymore. It is really up to my daughter to make the changes.

THERAPIST: Do you agree with that?

DAUGHTER: Yeah, I really need to do the work here.

Confidence scaling question

The confidence scaling question measures how confident clients are that change will occur. Again, this question can be asked in the active or passive voice:

Active: On a scale from 1 to 10, where 1 is that you have very little confidence that you will be able to solve these problems, and 10 is all the confidence in the world, even though you may not know how right now, where would you say you are on this scale?

Passive: On a scale from 1 to 10, where 1 is that you have very little confidence that these problems will be solved, and 10 is all the confidence in the world, where would you say you are on this scale?

With families and couples each person's confidence may be different. We sometimes ask clients to explain the difference in the numbers in order to clarify the goals.

THERAPIST: So Bob, you are a 7, and Mary, you're a 3.

BOTH: Correct.

THERAPIST: So Bob, what makes you so much more confident than Mary?

BOB: Well, I'm determined to make this work.

MARY: I'm burned out and at this point I need to see Bob make an effort.

THERAPIST: So Mary, when you see Bob making an effort, is this going to raise your confidence?

MARY: Maybe.

THERAPIST: What else would need to happen for your confidence to be higher? (*Notice the use of the passive version, because she is saying he needs to work first.*)

MARY: It's not that he never does anything, it's just that his effort does not last beyond a week.

THERAPIST: How long would it need to last for your confidence to come up just a little, to say a 4?

MARY: Maybe 2 weeks (*this is valuable information for Bob*).

Sometimes we ask a confidence question after the client has described a difficult next step. As the therapist you may sense that the client's next step, albeit small, is unlikely to happen given past history. In situations like this we ask a confidence question similar to this:

• *On a scale from 1 to 10, 1 being that you have no confidence that you will be able to accomplish this next step, and 10 being that you are absolutely sure you will do it, where are you?*

You can then follow up with a next step question on this confidence scale:

• *So if you are at a 1 for confidence now, what is one small thing that you can do to make yourself a little more confident?*

The client's answer to this question will probably lead you into a discussion about ideas and strategies. It is important to continue to make the client come up with the solutions.

Other scaling questions

At times it is very useful to develop other scales with our clients. Sometimes we will suggest another scale, but most often our clients define them. By encouraging clients to develop their own scales they learn how to self-monitor what they deem as important to them. Some examples are the following:

- *On a scale of 1 to 10, 10 being you feel great* (client's language), *and 1 is you are totally depressed, where would you say you are today?*

- *On a scale of 1 to 10, where 1 is you are not having any thoughts of hurting yourself (or others) and 10 is you are going to hurt yourself, where are you right now?* (Note: This scale is reversed because most hospitals and inpatient units reverse it in this manner.)

Even when clients are able to quantify their feelings in behavioral terms, there are times when creating a scale to measure progress is appropriate. For example, we had a family in which the parents felt like their daughter was using their house like a hotel, and the daughter felt like the parents did not want her to be at home. They developed the following scales:

For the parents: *On a scale of 1 to 10, 1 being just like a hotel, and 10 being like a home, how do you feel your daughter is treating your home?*

For the daughter: *On a scale of 1 to 10, where 1 is you do not feel welcome at all, and 10 is you feel very welcome in the house, how welcome do you feel?*

These were very useful in tracking the family's progress in a global way as they worked on individual goals related to these issues.

INTEGRATION ISSUES

Tracking responses to scaling questions. During the first session we ask all the clients in the room all three of these questions. We often draw a fast grid in our notes to track all the answers when there is more than one person in the room:

	Progress	**Willingness**	**Confidence**
Bob			
Mary			

Next Step: Bob

                    Mary

Next step. There are times when clients state that their next step is that someone else will do something. Depending on our level of rapport, the client's relationship to the problem and goal and who is in the room, we may or may not accept this as a doable next step. If we feel this is a setup for failure for the client, we may say, "That isn't in your control. Can you think of one small thing that you can do to move yourself to a 2.5?" or we may say, "So when he does that, what difference will that make for you?"

Managed behavioral health and scaling. There is another important use for the progress scaling question. We keep track of the answers that our clients give us, and write them in our session notes. We are then able to demonstrate progress by reporting the change on the progress scale to the case manager when we are reviewing treatment with a managed care company. We are also able to easily identify a next step in the treatment. In addition, when we are preparing our marketing materials and outcome data we are able to report average progress reported by clients. We track the answer to the progress scaling question in the first session and the last, subtract the two, and average these across clients' diagnostic categories and treatment modality (individual, couple, family, group).

When clients are stuck. The client may not know what the next step is when you ask the follow-up question to the progress scale. When we feel that the client is stuck in this fashion, we ask, *"So when you do know the next step, what will be different?"* or *"What will be some small sign that this is beginning to happen?"* There are times when we just need to sit with the fact that the client cannot think of what is going to make their situation just a little better.

Scaling with young children.   Some of our younger clients have difficulty with number lines. There are several alternatives we use:

- *Imagine that when you came here your school problem was this big* (can draw it as large, or use a wall height chart found in many pediatrician's offices), *and when the problem is solved enough it is this big* (small). *How big is it right now?*

- *If the problem that brought you here started as this big* (draw a pie) *and when it is solved enough that you do not need to be here it is this big* (draw pie with just the crumbs left), *how big is it right now?*

- *If the problems that brought you here today were this long* (use a piece of rope) *and when they are solved enough they are this long, how long would you say they are right now?*

- Use marbles and let the child take as many as represents the problem. Use colors, blocks smile and sad faces, clocks to scale throughout the course of the day (appropriate especially for inpatient programs). (All suggested by Boston therapists).

Clients in hospitals. It has been our experience that many hospitals utilize scaling questions as a way to measure decreasing symptoms. It is very helpful to continue to use scaling with clients recently discharged and important to remember that hospitals reverse the scale: 10 is often the worst that it can get. Our paradigm shift from focusing on problems to focusing on solutions has caused us to scale the presence of progress toward goals.

9

Ending the First Session

Prior to taking our consultation break, we ask the client one last question:

Is there anything else that I haven't asked about and that you feel I should know before I take a break and consult with the team (Berg & Miller, 1992)*?*

If you are not using a team you can say:

Is there anything else that I haven't asked about and that you feel I should know before I take a break and think about our meeting?

We view this as another invitation for clients to tell us information that we have not asked about. Most clients respond that there is nothing else. Some will bring up a new goal that needs to be explored, while others will tell you some fact they deem to be relevant to treatment. We believe that asking this question helps to maintain rapport with clients by sending the message that we have not heard it all, and are just starting to understand their world. It also reduces the occurrence of the "doorknob" effect (clients saying on their way out of your office, "Oh, by the way, did I tell you I was mandated to come here by the court?").

Consultation break

The consultation break is the one part of the Solution Focused model that practitioners have the most difficulty adapting to their own style of therapy. Few therapists are used to getting up out of their chairs and walking out of the room, leaving the client behind! Most therapists have been exposed to the idea of taking a consultation break in the context of family therapy, but few utilize the break outside of family therapy models. The Solution Focused model utilizes the consultation break toward the end of each session. The benefits of having the luxury to consult with a team that has been observing the session are obvious. Less obvious are the benefits of consulting with a colleague or team that was not watching the session and is not familiar with what has transpired. We utilize the consultation break in several different ways, depending on what is available to us in any particular setting:

- Leave the room and consult with a colleague or team.
- Leave the room and sit by ourselves.
- Leave the room and call a colleague.

When leaving the room is just not possible (you work at home, there is no other place for you to go, the client can not be left alone) we will stay in the room and tell our clients we are going to take a few minutes to review what they have told us and give them some feedback. We have had colleagues call us from all over the world to spend five minutes "teaming" with them. When we are working in a clinic we just walk around until we find an open door, pop our head in, and ask for a few minutes of our colleague's time.

Regardless of the format and make-up of your team, the purpose of the consultation break remains the same: to develop an intervention message to be delivered to the client. We view the break as very important. By leaving the room we are giving both ourselves and our clients some time to contemplate the session. There are many professions that utilize time away from clients in a similar manner: doctors, attorneys, mechanics, and others. Some clients have reported to us that they think the break is very respectful by sending the message that their problem is important and difficult enough that even the professional needs to take a few minutes to think about it. When we are using a team that has not observed the session, we try to present the following material to them:

- The nature of the problem
- The client-therapist-goal relationship
- Some aspects of the client's response to the miracle question
- Exceptions
- Answers to the scaling questions
- The client's next step

We have found it helpful to clarify ahead of time what you expect from the team during the break. Each clinician, depending on her therapeutic model, will want different feedback from the team during the break. We have experienced going into a team without first discussing the format, and in general chaos ensues. We make it clear that we are looking for those components outlined below to enable us to construct a good intervention message.

The intervention message

The intervention message (Berg & Miller, 1992) is what we say to our clients when we return from our break. Most of the time we have written it out so we do not omit or add any parts. Like the rest of the model, crafting intervention messages takes some practice. These do not need to be literary works; quite the opposite, they should be crafted incorporating as much of the client's language as possible (the exception would be if you are working with a literary genius). The intervention message has three components: validations, bridge, and task. Each intervention message will vary depending on the course of the session, your style, and the therapist-client-goal relationship. Below are the basics for creating an intervention message.

Validations: Validations consist of those statements to our clients that emphasize and encourage our clients' behaviors that are producing the results they want. By mentioning these behaviors at this time we are once again reinforcing them. We try to validate our clients' view of the situation and to normalize feelings, sometimes with some psychoeducation. It is important to incorporate our clients' language into the intervention message as much as possible. During this phase of the intervention message we want to create a "yes set" (Miller, 1992b). In a yes set, clients are literally nodding their heads up and down agreeing with what we are saying. For example:

> *THERAPIST*: This was a difficult session and you both
> worked hard here today. We feel that you were
> both very honest with us and each other, even
> though that was not always easy to do. We
> really felt like you were trying to work on the
> problem, and that you will continue to work on it
> when you leave here.

Bridge: The bridge is the rationale for asking the client to do the task. For example, when we are going to assign a task that the client has already mentioned she is doing, we might say:

> *THERAPIST*: Because you are on the right track...

Task: The task is what we are asking the client to do, notice, or think about between now and the next time we meet.

The task that we assign to a client, is determined by several factors. The chart below is an over-simplification of task development. For more information see Berg & Miller, 1992; Molnar & deShazer, 1987; and O'Hanlon & Weiner-Davis, 1989.

Relationship	Task
Customer-Seller Type Relationship	Do Task
Complainant-Listener Type Relationship	Notice Task
Visitor-Host Type Relationship	Invitation to Return

Do Tasks: As the name implies, when the client and therapist are in the customer-seller type relationship we can ask clients to do something between sessions. The most typical tasks we assign clients are these:

- Do their next step. (This refers to the progress scale.)
- Do more of what they are already doing that is working (this is for clients who talked about exceptions).
- Pretend their miracle happened.

Example of intervention message
with a customer-seller type relationship:

THERAPIST: This has been a difficult session and you have worked very hard today. There is a lot going on in your life right now, and we think it was a good idea for you to come in now and straighten things out. It is clear to us that you have given this a lot of thought and have already started to do things to improve your situation. We think you are right on target, and we agree with your next step, so between now and the next time we meet, we want you to do your next step and notice what difference it makes.

Notice Tasks: When we ask a client to do a notice task, the client-therapist-goal relationship is the complainant-listener type. The most typical notice tasks are these:

- Notice when things are going they way you would like them to, and what is different (adopted from the formula first session task, de Shazer, 1985).
- Notice when things are a little better.
- Notice when the problem is not a problem.
- Notice when pieces of the miracle happen.
- Notice exceptions to the problem.
- Notice when you are less depressed (if this is the client's language)

**Example of intervention message
with a complainant-listener type relationship:**

THERAPIST: This has been a hard session and you have both worked very hard today. We can understand your frustration with your son's behavior, and think it was a good idea to come in today. We are impressed that despite everything that has occurred, you are still willing to try and improve your relationship with your son. We also agree that you cannot control his behavior, and have to continue to find ways to "separate" (*their words*). To help you continue to do this, what we would like you to do between now and the next time we meet is to notice those times when things are going the way you would like them to go and notice what is different about those times – what you do differently and what your son does differently – so that we can talk about them.

Invitation to Return: On the rare occasion when a client and therapist remain in the visitor-host relationship throughout the session, there is only one task we can assign. We invite the client to return for another session.

Example of intervention with a visitor-host type relationship:

> *THERAPIST*: This has been a hard session and we appreciate your cooperation, even though it was not your idea to come here today. We understand how frustrating it must be to have to come in, talk to a complete stranger, and spend your time doing this, particularly when you do not think there is a problem. We agree with you that you need to continue to do what you can to keep your probation officer off your back, so we would like to invite you to come back in for another session.

Once we have given the intervention message, we typically ask our clients if they have any other questions, schedule the next appointment if there is going to be one, and finish the session.

INTEGRATION ISSUES

Using a team. Using a team takes some getting used to. You must rapidly evaluate what has transpired in the session, summarize this for the client, formulate validations, and craft a brilliant task all in the span of five minutes or less! When we first started using a team, we found it hard to complete any of this in a short period of time. What we discovered is that the other team members had their own ideas about what was going on in the room, and most therapists are used to "processing" when they gather as a group. We found it very useful to discuss (at a time when there was *not* a client waiting for us in our office) what our expectations of the break and team were, and how they could be the most useful to us at that time. It has taken some time to focus the team breaks so that we all work well together. We have found it possible, and in fact very helpful, to team with therapists who are not Solution Focused. These therapists tend to add different kinds of questions, and add insights to the session that get us thinking in a different way.

Over validating clients. It is important to evaluate before giving our intervention message (and at times during the delivery), whether we are "over validating" the client. Over validating is when the client is not engaged in a yes set (this could also mean that our validations are off base) or for whatever reason the client has a hard time accepting this kind of validation. In these cases we are careful to monitor clients' responses as we deliver the validation piece.

Giving a task to look for exceptions. At times our clients are able to report that there are exceptions to a problem, but they are not completely certain how these occur, and what part if any they play in the development of these exceptions. When the appropriate   client-therapist-goal relationship exists (either customer-seller or complainant-listener), we may ask our clients to notice the exceptions in an effort to discover any patterns that may exist.

Assigning multiple tasks.   As you think about the client-therapist-goal relationships you will find that you are giving different tasks to different family members. For example, you will give a "do task" to the willing child and a matching "notice" task to the frustrated parents or fed up teachers. A colleague who works in home based services told us about a father and son who weren't getting along. The son was in the customer relationship and the father was in the complainant relationship. She gave the following tasks: To the son she told him to do one thing each day that his father expected him to do that he doesn't usually do. To the father she asked him to try and notice if his son tries anything new. The son loved the task, partly because this meant his father would pay some attention to him. Interestingly enough the father was not excited about this task and the work was then focused on the father. In this case the father was supposed to spend his entire week looking for what his son was doing "right" instead of looking for the usual "bad" behavior. The message to the son was that his father was being asked to get involved also so the son wasn't the only one working on this problem. The message to the father was that his son wasn't the only one who would have to change his attitude. We find this is often the case with referral sources who present in the complainant relationship.

Utilizing the phone system. If you have the opportunity to utilize an intercom phone system during your sessions, you will find this helpful to staying on track and focused. We explain to the client that the team may buzz in during the session to recommend a different type of question or clarification of something the client just said. Many phone systems have this capability and can be easily adjusted to accommodate your needs. If you do not have a two-way mirror, you can also utilize a microphone system and/or a video camera through a small opening in a wall. There are many possibilities for creating the live team environment in different settings.

Running out of time. There have been times when we will be meeting with a client, our time will almost be up, and we have not yet asked the miracle question, or scaling; we consider this a productive session as well. It has been our experience that when the session does not progress at a similar pace to most others, it is because the client has a need to spend more time on the problem definition or the miracle. It could also mean that there were so many exceptions that termination was discussed. We will still take our break, and include in the intervention message a part that states that the next time we meet, we will begin to concentrate on what they want to be different in the future. Some clients may need a task to help them finish whatever "explaining" they need to so that they can move on to the next step. The following case scenario illustrates this:

Case Example: Joel is a 32-year-old male who has recently been discharged from an inpatient unit. When we begin the session I start by asking Joel, "What brings you here today?" Joel spends the next 40 minutes telling me about his recent hospitalization, the three hospitalizations prior to this one, and the development of his "troubles." I ask very few questions during this time, take a few notes, but mostly listen and acknowledge Joel's story. During the session I make a few attempts to change the tenor of the conversation to being more future oriented by asking Joel such questions as, "How will that be different in the future?" I also ask Joel how he would know that I had heard and understood enough of his story to be helpful to him. Joel is not ready to begin to explore the future until he is sure I understand the beginning of his story. The following is the intervention message that we give to Joel:

> *THERAPIST*: It is clear that you have been through a lot, and we have only begun to hear and understand your story and pain. As you said, you have survived a lot. We are impressed by your willingness to share what you have with us. We also think that there is more to your story that you feel we need to know so that we can begin to move forward. So between now and the next time we meet, what we would like you to do is think about, and write down if you think this would be helpful, what more we need to know.

Finishing the session. At the end of the first session we ask our clients if they want to come back, and if so, when. We do not make the assumption that clients will want to return, or that if they do, they will want to return in one week's time. We ask our clients how long they think they will need between sessions in order to achieve their next step (if they have a clear next step). The time between sessions for our clients runs a full range from those whom we see each week to others whom we only see four times a year.

There are other times that clients will automatically assume that they need to come back in one week. This may be due to a past therapy experience, or a general expectation of therapy. We will encourage our clients to think about this assumption. In this era of managed behavioral health care we will also discuss with our clients the limitations of their benefit and space the sessions out accordingly. There are times when we feel that we need to see the client in one week or less typically with suicidal and homicidal clients, and we will tell the client our reasons for wanting to meet so soon. We have found that if we see clients each week, there may be no time for improvement, or for the client to try something different. We firmly believe that the majority of the work done in therapy occurs outside of the therapy room. When we are working with multiple people, families, and other systems such as schools, one week is not enough time for significant changes to occur and be noticed by everyone. We have found that it may take longer (but care should be taken not to wait too long) for the change to be noticed.

Time between sessions. The time in between sessions varies from client to client. There are times when our needs will dictate how soon a client returns (as in the case of a client having suicidal ideation), but the vast majority of the time we ask our clients when they would like to return. We will sometimes preface the question with, "Usually between the first and second session there are one or two weeks; when do you feel you would like to come back?" As we will discuss later, we want to be careful not to see the client too soon. We have experienced situations when the client has been in therapy before and assumes that in order for therapy to work, or be "good therapy," we must meet weekly. We often discuss this belief with our clients and help them to see that it is not necessary to come to therapy each week.

We have also seen clients who request returning in one week's time because there is some urgency to the work they are doing. It may be that they are under a time constraint to resolve a problem. Some clients request returning in a week's time as a means of "proving" to their partners that they were actually working on the problems. During later sessions we spend some time discovering other ways for these clients to prove this to their partners.

Making the model meet the client.   Although we have presented this first session material in a specific order, you will find after practicing these questions that there are sessions in which you do not ask every question or adhere to this specific order. Here are several examples.

- As we mentioned earlier, some new clients begin a session by saying something like, "I am not sure I need to be here anymore." Sometimes clients have waited a long period of time for an appointment and have already started solving their problems. In this case we begin with exceptions and move to scaling.

- In some cases clients who present as extremely depressed cannot answer the miracle question. We will enter into a "coping sequence" (Berg & Miller, 1992) (see Chapter 11). We will also move to scaling after we have explored any exceptions. We will also elicit other scales that the client may find helpful.

- When a client is being transferred from another therapist because treatment was unsuccessful, or when we do consultations for managed care companies, we tend to begin with scaling questions. We will ask, "On a scale from 1 to 10, 1 being when you first began treatment for this problem and 10 being when it is solved enough that you don't need to be in treatment anymore, where are you right now?" (deShazer, 1994). This will give us an idea of what was helpful about their previous treatment and where they may be stuck. It also acknowledges the previous work and honors that relationship.

What clients do while we are taking a break. During the break clients are often just sitting quietly and thinking about what we have discussed. Others read a magazine, and couples and families will often talk or just hold hands. During the first session clients do not really know what to expect when we return from the break. Many are leaning forward in anticipation; others are more defensive in their postures, sitting with their arms folded. One adolescent client sighed loudly after the intervention message and said, "Whew, I thought you were going to yell at me."

Gathering history.   In some cases we decide that we need to refer the client for a psychiatric evaluation, or our agency requires certain problem-focused information after a first session.   In either case, we take the opportunity before our break to let the client know we need to ask some questions that may or may not have anything to do with treatment.   In the beginning of the session we have told our clients that we may do this so it is not a surprise.   We believe it is important to distinguish this type of questioning from the rest of the Solution Focused interview (see Chapter 12).

A full session

Renee is a 30-year-old female who was referred by a relative's therapist. During the intake call she stated that she has had a problem with alcohol in the past and has seen other therapists and not found them helpful. Renee stated on the phone that she is taking Prozac and Xanax.   From the Client Information Form (see Chapter 13) we learned that both of her parents have issues with alcohol, and she has identified 23 of 32 problems on the bottom of the page that apply to her or her family.   The following is a partial transcript of the first session, beginning after the treatment and fee agreement has been signed.

> *THERAPIST*: So, why don't you tell me what brings you here today?
>
> *CLIENT*: Well, I was married for five years and had a daughter. Right now we are getting divorced. I don't have a job, Youth Services has custody of my child, and I am coming out of a bad relationship. I have panic attacks (*pause*), and have been taking Prozac for three years.
>
> *THERAPIST*:   Sounds like a lot of stress (*client nods*). How often do you have panic attacks?
>
> *CLIENT*: The last one was two weeks ago. They happen every two or three weeks.

THERAPIST: Okay, you just ended a relationship, your child is with Youth Services; are there other things that brought you here today?

CLIENT: Well, I just ended a really bad relationship (*begins to cry*), and I just don't know where to go from here. No one, except my brother and sister-in-law, is supportive.

THERAPIST: Okay.

CLIENT: I just want to stop everything. I have had a drinking problem in the past, and don't want to start again. If it weren't for my brother, I'd be drinking now. (*Client stops and cries for a few seconds.*) I just want to feel better.

THERAPIST: Of course. There are a lot of things going on here, so in order for me to get a handle on it I want to ask you an unusual question. Suppose tonight, after our session, you go home and fall asleep, and while you are sleeping a miracle happens. The miracle is that the problems that brought you here today are solved. But you don't know that the miracle has happened because you are asleep. When you wake up in the morning, what will be some of the first things you will notice that will be different to tell you this miracle has happened?

CLIENT: I don't understand. How will I know?

THERAPIST: Right, you wake up and all day tomorrow and the next few days and weeks you'll know that this miracle happened. What will you notice different to let you know that this miracle has happened?

CLIENT: Well, I guess I would gain some control over my life...(*thinks for a while*)...and not be in a relationship with people who are trying to control me.

THERAPIST: Okay, so you will gain some control over your life, not be in that kind of relationship. What else will be different?

CLIENT: Maybe I would feel like I have some direction in my life. I would get to see my daughter more, and maybe feel like I have accomplished something.

THERAPIST: Good, what else?

CLIENT: I'm not sure...I'd feel like I was making it on my own. Also, there wouldn't be any grudges in the family, and I would know that everything is not my fault, I'd feel better about myself.

THERAPIST: Okay, let me go back to a few of the things you said. When you feel like you have some control over your life, what will be different?

CLIENT: Everything will be different, I will be able to make it on my own, I'll be able to think clearly, and things will just be calmer like the past two weeks have been (*spontaneous exception*).

THERAPIST: What have the past two weeks been like? (*The therapist could also have continued with the miracle here and gone back later to this exception.*)

CLIENT: After I left the jerk, I moved in with my brother and they have been great. I've even been happy a few times.

THERAPIST: How did you do that?

CLIENT: I think it is being in a place that I know what to expect and it actually happens. When someone says they are going to do something, they do.

THERAPIST: So when you are in a place that is predictable, you feel better?

CLIENT: Yes.

THERAPIST: What are the signs to you that you are feeling better?

CLIENT: I'm more cheerful. When I get out of bed in the morning, I don't mind and I am neater.

THERAPIST: Okay, so moving in with your brother was a good move on your part.

CLIENT: Definitely.

THERAPIST: What other pieces of the miracle do you feel have already begun to happen, even if it is just a little?

CLIENT: I got out of a bad relationship.

THERAPIST: How did you decide to do that?

CLIENT: I had no choice, it was really bad for me. If I didn't get out I don't know what I would have done.

THERAPIST: So getting out was really a way of taking care of yourself (*reframe*)?

CLIENT: Yes. (*We amplified and reinforced this more before moving on to scaling.*)

THERAPIST: So, on a scale from 1 to 10, 1 being the problems that brought you here today were at their worst, and 10 being when they are solved enough that you do not need to be here anymore, where would you say you are right now?

CLIENT: Hm...maybe a 3.

THERAPIST: Okay, so if you are at a 3 right now, what do you need to do to be able to say you are a 3.5?

CLIENT: I think I'd have to get a job.

THERAPIST: That seems like a big step, maybe more like an 8.

CLIENT: Or 11!

THERAPIST: What would be the first step in getting a new job?

CLIENT: Well, I've already been on a few interviews, and put applications in at a few places.

THERAPIST: You have?

CLIENT: Yes.

THERAPIST: How did you do that?

CLIENT: I just knew I had to start to get up on my own feet.

THERAPIST: Okay, so what is the next step in getting a job?

CLIENT: I guess just keep doing what I am going.

THERAPIST: How are you going to do that?

CLIENT: You mean continue to look for a job?

THERAPIST: Yes.

CLIENT: Just keep doing what I have been.

THERAPIST: Okay.

CLIENT: There is one thing that I am concerned about.

THERAPIST: What is that?

CLIENT: My mood. I feel like it has been all over the place.

THERAPIST: Okay. How would you like it to be instead?

CLIENT: Consistent.

THERAPIST: Okay, on a scale from 1 to 10, 1 being not consistent and 10 being very consistent, how consistent is your mood these days?

CLIENT: Maybe between a 4 and an 8; it depends on the day.

THERAPIST: Okay, that was important information for me to have. Let me ask you a few more numbers questions...(*We asked willingness and confidence scaling questions*).

THERAPIST: I need to ask you some questions that may or may not have anything to do with why you are here, but I need the information for my records. (*Asked questions about eating, sleeping, concentration, energy level, domestic violence, past and present medications, etc.*).

THERAPIST: Is there anything else you think I need to know before I take my break?

CLIENT: No, I don't think so.

THERAPIST: Okay, I'll be back in a few minutes.

BREAK

THERAPIST: You have been through a lot, and have been under a lot of stress, and we probably don't know the half of it. We agree that you have already started to take some steps in the right direction by being able to face the day, have already begun looking for a job, and have left an abusive relationship. Another sign to us that you have a direction is that you know you need to figure out who you are, so that you can be the mom you want to be *(another goal she mentioned during her miracle)*. This is a goal that you are already working on. We also agree that it is important that you know and remind yourself that it is not all your fault. It takes some understanding about yourself to ask for and take help from someone, and this is a sign that you are beginning to like yourself more and raise your self-esteem *(another goal from her miracle)*. Considering that you are already doing several things, that we agree are steps in the right direction, we think you should keep doing what you are doing. Assuming you would like to come back, what we would like you to do between now and the next time we meet is to notice when things are a little better for you.

The above case example illustrates many of the key components of a first session. First sessions typically take 50-60 minutes and large families can take an hour and a half. As a reminder, first sessions do not always follow this format and it is important to remember to follow the client. We will now focus on later sessions.

10

Later Sessions: Amplifying Improvement

When clients return for a later session, one of the main goals is to discover with our clients what has been working and improving between sessions. Again, all of the questions that we ask reflect our assumptions. In preparation for later sessions we usually review our notes from the previous session, or the tape if one was made. We notice, and often write down and take into the session with us, the client's answer to the progress scale and next step from the previous session. In addition, we review the goals and the client-therapist-goal relationship. In the rare case that we have not asked the miracle question in the first session, we would begin with this in the second session. Although it is not a "rule," a typical later session will flow as follows:

- What's Better?
- E.A.R.S.
- Scaling
- Is There Anything Else?

- Break
- Intervention Message

What's better?

The first question that we pose to our clients is, *"What's been better?"* Most clients are typically not anticipating this question, and therefore it can take them some time to warm up. There are times when clients will respond that they do not know what is better, or will say "Nothing." It is important to give our clients some time to think before moving on in our questioning. "I don't know" can be a knee-jerk response. We often ask our clients to "think about it for a second."

There are basically two scenarios that develop when we ask the "what's better" question:

- Things are better.
- Things are not better.

We will begin with what we typically do when the client's situation has improved and deal with the harder scenario of when things are not better in the next chapter. It is important to remember that the improvement we are referring to as "better" is most often *not* dramatic, but quite the opposite. The change that we most often discuss with clients is small, and at times hardly noticeable. It is for this very reason that we methodically ask about and explore even the smallest of changes, regardless of whether they were deliberate or random.

When things are better

Berg and Miller (1992) created an acronym for the process of discovering with a client what has been better that we have found very useful in reminding us of all the details we should be drawing out of the client.   The acronym is E.A.R.S., and it stands for Elicit, Amplify, Reinforce, and Start Over.

Elicit: One of the first questions that we ask our clients in later sessions is:

- *What's been better?*
- *What's better?*
- *It's been _____ weeks since we last met, what's better?*

This is done to elicit what has been better for the client(s).

> *THERAPIST*: So, since our last session, what's been
>   better?
> *CLIENT*: Better?
> *THERAPIST*: Better.
> *CLIENT*: Well, let me think about that. I did go to school
>   more last week.

In some cases you may have spoken to a client who was in crisis in between sessions. It would probably feel inappropriate to ask, "since we met what's better?"   Instead we would ask, "since we spoke what's better?" or "since we spoke how have you coped?" or "since we spoke what have you figured out?"

Amplify: Once a client has articulated what has been better we try to find out as much information as possible about what has been better. Depending on rapport and our own style, we may or may not be very enthusiastic at times. The bold sections in the example below are typical questions that we ask to amplify what is better.

> *(Continued from above)*
> *THERAPIST*: You went to school more?!
> *CLIENT*: Yes.
> *THERAPIST*: **How much more**?

CLIENT: Well, I was able to get to school everyday this week, and three of the days I was even on time.

THERAPIST: Wow! **How did you do that?**

CLIENT: I just went.

THERAPIST: You just went? Did you do anything differently so that you did go?

CLIENT: Well, I did start to set my alarm on my own, and I moved it to my desk across the room.

THERAPIST: Great idea, **how was that helpful?**

CLIENT: I have to get out of bed to turn it off.

THERAPIST: Brilliant. So you went to school more; **what difference did this make in the problems that brought you here?**

CLIENT: My parents are off my back a little.

THERAPIST: Really, **what have you noticed?**

CLIENT: Well, they just yelled less.

THERAPIST: And when they yelled less **what do you think they noticed different about you**?

CLIENT: I know because they commented that I was less moody and hanging around them more, which is what they wanted.

THERAPIST: **Who else noticed** that you went to school more?

CLIENT: My friends (*laughing*)!

THERAPIST: **What did they notice?**

CLIENT: That I was there.

THERAPIST: **Who else noticed?**

CLIENT: Two of my teachers were real nice and told me they would stay after school and help me make up work.

THERAPIST: So was getting to school a step in the right direction for you (*client's language*)?

CLIENT: Definitely.

THERAPIST: **What will it take for you to continue to do this**?

CLIENT: Well, I have to keep telling myself I have to get
   up each day, and going to bed earlier would help.
THERAPIST: Good, that makes sense. So you were able
   to get to school more; **what else was better?**

To summarize, when we are amplifying what the client has done better, or
what has been better, we typically ask:

* *What have you noticed that is better?*
* *When did this happen?*
* *Who else noticed?*
* *How did they respond?*
* *What do you think they noticed different about you?*
* *What difference did that make in your relationship?*
* *How do you explain that this happened?*
* *How did you know to do that?*
* *How can you get this to happen more?*

Reinforce: It is very important to reinforce what our clients are doing to
make the situation improve. We do this both verbally and nonverbally.
Verbally we say things like, *"That's great,"* *"You did what?"* and *"Say
that again!"* Nonverbally we nod, look excited, smile, make eye contact
with our clients, and write down what they are saying. We continue with
this process for as long as our clients report more things that are better, or
we run out of time.   Dr. Scott D. Miller (1992b) has a wonderful
technique of getting clients to repeat what they have been doing to make
things better, or what they have been doing better.   Based on this
technique we might ask a client, *"So your parents yelled less, you went to
school on time, and what was the third thing you said was better?"* This
makes clients state again, and hear in their own voice again, what has
been better.

Start over: Once this particular sequence of questions has been exhausted,
we begin the process over again, by asking, *"What else has been better?"*

Is the progress related to the goal?

At this point in the session we want to ask ourselves, and the client if need be, "Are these changes related to the client's goals?" If we are not sure, we ask the client:

- *Are these the types of changes you would like to see continue in your life?*
- *What difference did these changes make for you?*
- *How are they helpful?*

If the changes are related to the goal, then we feel comfortable proceeding to scaling questions. If the changes are not related, we often ask the client about this with some curiosity. For example:

> *THERAPIST*: I'm confused. You said that your week was better, but that nothing has really changed in your relationship with your husband (*our understanding of her goal*). How do you explain this?

or

> *THERAPIST*: So your son went to school more, and yet things are not better? What do you think about that?

It may be that our clients need for the changes to happen more in order to recognize that things are indeed getting better. We might ask the parent whose son went to school more:

> *CLIENT:* Well, it was only a week and probably a fluke, so I don't want to get my hopes up only to be disappointed again.
>
> *THERAPIST:* So, you would feel like things are getting better when your son continues going to school or he continues trying?

CLIENT: That's a good question...I think I would
           actually just need to see him trying in order to
           feel like it's worth getting my hopes up. I guess I
           was kind of excited when he went to school, but I
           have been down this road before with him and
           this time I want to help him keep it going.
THERAPIST: Okay, I can understand that. What do you
           think you can do, if anything, to help him without
           doing it for him?

CLIENT: You understand my dilemma. It's not that I
        don't want to be supportive, but I also don't want
        to make the same mistakes over again and do it
        for him, which doesn't work in the long run.

At this point the parent is talking about things being better and her
concerns about how she can support him without doing it for him. She
may still need to see him working on this for a longer period of time
before she will have confidence that it is a more lasting change, but at
least she has shifted to a more positive notice and support position. We
might also start scaling her confidence that her son will continue to try to
work on this issue.

Scaling in later sessions

At this point in the session we ask scaling questions. Scaling in
later sessions is very similar to scaling in the first session. The primary
functions of scaling in later sessions is to track progress, establish the next
small step, and know when it is time to terminate.

We always ask the progress scale:

- *On a scale from 1 to 10, where 1 is when the problems that brought
  you here were at their worst and 10 is when they are solved enough*

that you do not need to be here anymore, where would you say you are right now?

and the follow-up (next step) question either in the active or passive voice:

- Active: *If you are at a 3 now, what do you think you need to do to say you are a 3.5 or a 4?*

- Passive: *If you are at a 3 now, what needs to happen for you to be able to say you are at a 3.5 or 4?*

When the client's answer to the progress scale is 7 or higher, we ask the confidence scaling question in either the active or the passive voice. (Note: the number 7 is arbitrary. We have decided on 7 based on our experience; yours may vary.)

- Active: *On a scale from 1 to 10, 1 being no confidence at all and 10 being all the confidence in the world that you will be able to maintain these changes, how confident are you?*

- Passive: *On a scale from 1 to 10, 1 being no confidence at all and 10 being all the confidence in the world that these changes will continue, how confident are you?*

It is not uncommon to have a client who is high on the progress scale but low on the confidence scale. For example:

> *THERAPIST*: So on a scale from 1 to 10, 1 being when the problems that brought you here were at their worst and 10 being when these problems are solved enough that you don't need to be here anymore, where would you both say you are today?
>
> *DAUGHTER*: 8.

MOTHER: Yes, I would agree with that. She has been doing really well and trying. She has gone to school, and been there on time most days.

THERAPIST: Okay, how confident are you that this situation will continue to improve?

DAUGHTER: 8.

MOTHER: 2.

DAUGHTER: Mom, that's not fair!

MOTHER: Sorry, but I've been here before, and it does not last. As soon as we get into therapy she works real hard, changes, and then it fades.

DAUGHTER: I think it will be different this time.

THERAPIST: What will need to happen to convince you that your daughter is not going to let it fade?

MOTHER: If she can just continue the effort.

THERAPIST: So how long will she need to continue the effort before you start to believe that it will last?

MOTHER: I'm not sure. Maybe another month.

THERAPIST: Do you think you can do that?

DAUGHTER: Yes, I do.

THERAPIST: What is it going to take to keep this going?

DAUGHTER: I just have to continue to remind myself that I have to work on it. It is also really helpful when my mom tells me I am doing well.

THERAPIST: Did you hear that, Mom?

MOTHER: Absolutely!

If we have developed any other scales with the client, we ask them at this point.

When both progress and confidence are above a 7 or 8, we can then ask the client:

- *Is there anything else that you would like to work on with me at this time?*

This is an invitation to clients to bring up any new issues or unresolved issues that they would like to talk about before we terminate.   If there are no other goals, then our work is complete.   If the client identifies new goals, we start over by redefining the goals.

Starting on a new goal

When clients report that they are high on the progress scale, and high on the confidence scale that they will be able to maintain this progress, they may also have a new goal. This new goal can be related to the original or not. At times clients are now ready to tackle harder issues that for a multitude of reasons they chose not to address earlier in their treatment. When a client starts with a new goal, we typically do not ask the miracle question again, but rather begin with the types of questions that would immediately follow the miracle question.

The new goal should be well formed and clients should begin to describe what will be different in their lives when this goal is achieved.

Case Example: Carol, a 16-year-old female, has successfully solved a problem with her boyfriend.

> *THERAPIST*: So are there other things that you would like to work on with me at this time?
>
> *CAROL*: Well, there is another issue that I would like to address.
>
> *THERAPIST*: Okay.
>
> *CAROL*: I want to figure out a way to get my mom off my back.
>
> *THERAPIST*: What do you mean?
>
> *CAROL*: Every time I want to leave the house, she grills me; where am I going, who is going to be there, what are we going to do, how long will I be there. She does this in front of my friends too, it's so embarrassing!
>
> *THERAPIST*: So when this is no longer a problem, what will be different?

CAROL: I don't know, maybe she would trust me, and just let me go out and not ask a thousand questions all the time.

THERAPIST: So your mom would trust you?

CAROL: Yeah.

THERAPIST: Do you feel like she trusts you now?

CAROL: Yeah, some.

THERAPIST: What are some examples of how she already trusts you?

CAROL: Well, she does let me go out sometimes after I tell her, convince her, I am not going to get mugged or arrested.

THERAPIST: How do you do that?

CAROL: How do I do what?

THERAPIST: How do you convince her that you are going to be okay?

CAROL: I tell her what I am going to do and just answer her questions.

THERAPIST: I see. So when she trusts you more what will be different?

CAROL: We won't get into fights about me going out.

THERAPIST: So when you are not fighting about you going out, what are you doing instead?

CAROL: Just getting along.

THERAPIST: What do you think your mother would say would need to be different in order for her to trust you more, and let you go out more?

CAROL: Hm....She would probably say I would have to be perfect! Not get into trouble. She got really mad when the police brought me home that one time; since then she grills me.

THERAPIST: So you would have to not get into trouble; what else?

CAROL: Go where I said I'm going to. But sometimes we change our minds!

THERAPIST: On a scale of 1 to 10, 10 being your mom
trusts you completely, where would you say
things are right now, today?

CAROL: Maybe a 4.

THERAPIST: Okay. What is one small thing that you
could do to make it a 4.5? Really small.

CAROL: Maybe call her the next time we change our
minds.

THERAPIST: That sounds great. What will it take for
you to do that?

CAROL: Hm...Maybe I'll tell Jackie *(friend)* to remind
me the next time.

To summarize, the types of questions that we ask when establishing a new
goal:

* *Are there other things that you would like to work on with me now?*
* *Are there other things your partner [mother, teacher, probation
officer] wants you to work on?*
* *So when this is no longer a problem, what will be different?*
* *What are some examples of when this is already happening?*
* *What would it take for you to do this more?*
* *Who needs to notice these changes in order for you to want to do
them more?*

Break and intervention message in later sessions

Just as in a first session, we encourage clinicians to take a break
in later sessions as well. During the later sessions the break becomes
easier for both therapist and client since both are more accustomed to the
procedure. The intervention message is composed of the same three
components as in the first session: validations, bridge, and task (see
Chapter 9). The development of an intervention message and task in a
later session in which the client reports progress is not complicated. We
simply reinforce what the client is doing that is working, and agree with
his next step if he has one. We will often give an additional task of

noticing when things are continuing to improve, or noticing what difference doing the next step makes.

Intervention Message for Carol (see above):

> *THERAPIST*:   You worked really hard today. Although we did not talk a lot about it, we want to make sure you pat yourself on the back for dealing with the problem with your boyfriend. You worked hard and made some tough decisions. We agree with you that trust between you and your mom is a major issue. We also think your next step in building this trust is a good one. So, assuming you want to come back, what we would like you to do is to try your next step, and notice what difference it makes.

INTEGRATION ISSUES

What to do if things are better, but the client is not sure of the next step. We typically ask clients what will be a small sign to them that things are a little better than where they are right now. Again, this is asking about what will be different, not how will they get there. If they continue to be unsure about the next step, we "sit with this."

Knowing when it is time to stop. Most often our clients are the ones who tell us that they no longer need to be in therapy. These are the clients who come in for the last session and know it is the last session. There are other times when clients will rate themselves high on the progress scale (above a 7) and high on the confidence scale (above a 7) and still want to come back. We believe this is worth exploring with the client. We find that clients do not necessarily need to make another appointment, but rather, they want to know that they can return in the future. It is important for us to explain that by not returning for a few weeks or a month does not mean that they have given up their "time slot." We will support our clients' needs, which may include a follow-up phone call in the future. There are also times when clients do not begin a session knowing it will be the last, but after E.A.R.S. and scaling they realize that they have either met their goals or made significant progress and no longer needs us to maintain their progress. We usually ask, "*So considering how high you are on the progress and confidence scales, do you think we need to meet anymore?*" The final scenario is when clients do not return, and do not communicate to us that they no longer need our services. We have found it important to not assume that it is treatment failure when clients do not return. Instead, we have adopted the practice of calling or writing to our clients to inquire as to why they have stopped. What we have discovered is that a large number of these clients stop coming because they no longer need our services.

In other cases our clients may want to stop for a period of time and then may or may not return to therapy. Very often when we are seeing a child for a school-related problem and school ends, there is no longer a need for us to continue to meet at that time. During the last session, we explain to the child and the parent that when school resumes in the fall they can begin with us again if they feel the need.

When things are different, but not better. There are times when clients report that things are different in their lives, but not necessarily better yet. For example, the wife who comes in for a later session and states that she has had a very difficult week, because she has decided to leave her husband. She is not noticing that her life is easier, or that she is happier, but her situation is very different. Many clients come into therapy to make difficult and life-altering decisions. It is important to remind our clients that they are on a path toward a goal, despite the fact that they are not noticing dramatic change at the present time. It is sometimes helpful to challenge clients to make the connections between their difficult decision and their ultimate goal.

11

Later Sessions: When Things Are Not Better

At times our clients come in and report that things are not better, and at times their situations are worse. When a client responds to the question, *"What's been better?"* with "Nothing" or "Things are worse" it is important for us to *remember not to panic.* This does not mean that the model does not work, we have failed, or we should transfer the person to another, more competent therapist.

Our first task is to determine if in fact things were better or different, but for some reason this is not foremost in the client's mind. We have experienced several different scenarios:

- A couple comes in and their relationship is better, but they had a fight on the way to our session.
- A client has made great advancement between sessions, but has experienced a death in the family.

- Things have remained the same in one area where they have been looking for improvement, and they have missed the changes in another area.
- A severely depressed client has not yet learned how to notice the small changes and needs to practice connecting thoughts with actions. Over time people usually can learn to focus on when things are slightly better instead of feeling depressed. They are still depressed, just less so.

The following example illustrates how we determine if things have improved or changed when the client initially reports that things are not better.

> *THERAPIST*: Since we last met, what's been better?
>
> *CLIENT*: Nothing. I think I am worse.
>
> *THERAPIST*: Why don't you tell me what has been happening over the past week.
>
> *CLIENT*: Well, I tried what we talked about, but nothing changed.
>
> *THERAPIST*: So, you tried something different?
>
> *CLIENT*: Yes.
>
> *THERAPIST*: How did you manage to try something different?
>
> *CLIENT*: I don't know. I guess I thought about it and decided I had nothing to lose at this point. We were in the middle of another fight and I just stopped yelling and sat down. He was so surprised that he stopped yelling. Then I calmly asked him if the yelling was helping and he looked confused and said "no." So I suggested that maybe we should try dealing with this a different way. I asked him what he thought we should do and then we had this great talk, but it didn't last. The next day we were fighting again and I was scared all over again.

THERAPIST: So let me get this straight. In the middle of
this heated argument you stopped and actually
calmed down enough to try something different?

CLIENT: Yeah.

THERAPIST: Not only did you stop and try something
different but it made him stop, calm down, and
listen. How did you decide to do this?

CLIENT: I had just had enough and I guess I want it to
work, and I know if we try hard enough things
can be okay again.

THERAPIST: So when it worked, were you surprised?

CLIENT: Yeah. I couldn't believe it.

THERAPIST: What do you think he thought?

CLIENT: Well, that was part of our talk. He admitted
that he never would have calmed down if I hadn't
done it first. I was surprised that he admitted
this.

To summarize, we ask the following types of questions to determine if
things are better:

- *Tell me about the week.*
- *What happened?*
- *What did you learn?*
- *What have you figured out?*

By asking these questions most of the time we discover that things really
are better, even if the "better" part is very small. We are not trying to
convince our clients that things are better, we are trying to help them look
for what may have been better. We definitely see a variety of clients who
do not improve between the first few sessions. However, once we begin
to get positive responses to these questions, we proceed as outlined in the
previous chapter, starting with E.A.R.S.

When things really are not better, it is important for us to resist
the temptation to explain the lack of progress. It is at this stage in the
therapeutic process that we often find ourselves sitting around staff

meetings talking about resistance, denial, and our client's inability to change due to the client being codependent, borderline, or drug dependent. Although these conversations are often interesting, we have not found them helpful with meeting the client's goals. What we have found productive is to think and talk with our team and the client about what we can do differently.

Do something different

There are several things we try to examine or do differently when treatment is not working (this means that the client is not reporting progress). We do this based on the following assumption: "If it does not work, try something else." This is one example of applying the model to the model. If after working with clients for a few sessions they are not reporting change, it does not make sense to continue to work in exactly the same manner. We will start to do something different.

Examine the goals. We often review the goals with ourselves, our colleagues, and most importantly with our clients to be certain that we are working on a well-formed goal. Many times we discover that we have not been working on the client's goal at all. For example:

Case Example: The following 16-year-old client was recently released from a seven-day hospitalization:

> *THERAPIST*: So, what's been better since you went home?
> *CLIENT*: Nothing, the hospital was stupid. All they did was change my medication.
> *THERAPIST*: How has school been since you got back?
> *CLIENT*: About the same. All they want me to do is talk about my hospitalization and "process." It's so stupid. I just wish they would all just get off my back.
> *THERAPIST*: How have things been at home?

CLIENT: Worse, my parents are all over me.

THERAPIST: From what they said to me, they are really worried about you hurting yourself again.

CLIENT: Yeah sure.

THERAPIST: Well, things do not seem to be getting better.

CLIENT: Nope.

THERAPIST: I was wondering something. We have been meeting for a while now, and things don't seem to be getting any better (*client nods*). All this time we have been working on school, and your behavior at home, and not hearing voices. I am curious, are any of those things that you want to be working on?

CLIENT: No, well maybe not hearing the voices, but as long as I stay on the medication, that's fine.

THERAPIST: Hm, well, what is it that you want?

CLIENT: I just want everyone to get off my back and leave me alone.

THERAPIST: That sounds like a great idea.

CLIENT: It would be wonderful, but it will never happen.

THERAPIST: What do you think it would take for everyone to get off your back?

CLIENT: I have no idea.

THERAPIST: So when everyone is off your back, what will be different?

CLIENT: Well, I won't have to come here anymore, sorry.

THERAPIST: No need to be sorry.

CLIENT: I just want to take a break from therapy for a while. I know I'll need to go again, but I want it to be my idea, not everyone else's.

THERAPIST: Okay, so what would you need to do to convince everyone that you don't need to be here anymore?

CLIENT: Good question.

THERAPIST: Who do you need to convince?

CLIENT: My case worker and my parents.

THERAPIST: Okay. I don't know your new case worker but I am hoping we will talk next week. For now let's concentrate on your parents. What would they need to see you do differently, so that you do not need to be here anymore?

CLIENT: I'm not really sure. I have been fine at home. I'm even keeping my curfew, but they still think that I need to be here.

THERAPIST: Okay.

CLIENT: The only reason that they say that is because the old case worker told them to keep me in therapy.

THERAPIST: Well, what do you think?

CLIENT: I think as long as I am not hearing voices and I'm following the rules, I shouldn't have to come.

THERAPIST: Okay. Here are some rules about the medication you are on. This agency has a policy that if you are on medication, you have to be in therapy. But you and I can decide how often we need to meet.

CLIENT: Okay.

THERAPIST: How often do you think we need to meet to satisfy your parents?

CLIENT: No idea, my mom's in the waiting room, why don't we ask her?

THERAPIST: Great idea.

(*Mother comes into the session.*)

THERAPIST: Well, we have been talking about your daughter coming to sessions less frequently. How has she been at home?

MOTHER: Fine. Since school ended, we have had no
  problems.

THERAPIST: That's what Emma (*the daughter*) said.
  Well, how long in between sessions will feel
  comfortable for you?

MOTHER: I'm not sure. What would you suggest?

THERAPIST: Well, given the medication, I would feel
  okay about every six weeks. How does that
  sound to you?

CLIENT: I can live with that. If after six weeks things
  are fine and I still don't hear voices, can we skip
  the appointment and make another?

THERAPIST: That would be fine with me. What do you
  think, Mom?

MOTHER: Okay I guess. What happens if something
  does go wrong?

THERAPIST: You can always call me.

It became very clear during this session that we had been pursuing goals
that were not salient to the client. Having the discussion that we did
helped to clarify many points and helped us to begin to work on the
client's goals.

Examine the client-therapist-goal relationship.   We find that many
times when things are not getting better it is because we have assumed
that the client-therapist-goal relationship is a customer-seller type, when in
fact, for that goal it is really a complainant-listener type. When we make
the wrong assumption about the nature of this relationship, we often
assign the wrong task, and ask questions about goals in which the client
may not be invested. One sign we look for is when we, the clinicians, are
feeling frustrated, and may be expecting our client to "do" something as if
the client were in the customer-seller type relationship for that goal and
the client is actually in the complainant-listener type relationship. In this
case we will pay attention to whether or not the client answers scaling
questions in the active or passive voice. Another sign is when we feel that

we are working harder than our clients, especially if we feel like we are trying to convince them of something. In this case we will reevaluate this relationship and maybe begin to challenge the clients' assumptions instead of trying to convince them that their perspective is wrong.

Listen more carefully to the client. We ask ourselves if we have been working on our own agenda or reading between the lines of what the client is saying to us. Steve deShazer (1994) states, "The danger of reading between the lines is that there might be nothing there. So, you've just got to listen to what the client says" (deShazer, 1994, p. 109). So if we think we have not been listening, we will make an extra effort to listen more carefully to the client's responses. Sometimes the client does not answer our question, but answers the question we should have asked. We try to figure out what question the client just answered so we can follow the client's needs.

Change the room. This sounds so simple, and it is. Changing the room or even the chair you sit in can have a profound effect on clients. When we teach in schools (graduate or others) we will sometimes ask students to change seats in the middle of class and take a different view of things.

Change the frequency. Sometimes if we meet too soon the client has not had enough of an opportunity to try something different. In other cases we have allowed too much time in between sessions and the client needs more support/less time in between sessions. We will let the client know we think this is something we should change and let the client determine when we should meet next.

Change the time. We have found that the time of day that we meet with our clients can effect the outcome of our meetings. If several sessions have gone by with the client reporting no progress, we try changing the time of day that we meet.

Change the day. We have also found that changing the day that we meet can have an effect. For example, while meeting with a family on a Friday only produced complaints about the son's poor performance over the school week, meeting with them on Monday allowed them to talk about what the son did well over the weekend.

Use a team or do not use a team. Depending on the therapeutic setting, there are times when utilizing a live team or taking the break (which we encourage using all the time) can make the difference. Utilizing a team can create the commitment for both client and therapist to stick to the goals, and add new questions or information to a session.

Request a psychiatric consultation. If we are working with someone who over the course of treatment has become depressed, or someone who was resistant to medication initially, or any other situation which may suggest the utilization of medication we will refer the client to a psychiatrist. Our view is that we do what works.

Ask the client to do something different. When clients report that nothing has improved by the third session (nothing means nothing, not even a small difference) or things have gotten worse, we will discuss this very directly with clients. We let our clients know that we will not continue to do things exactly the same way and that we will do something different. The exception to this policy is when clients are experiencing an acute or specific crisis that explains the lack of progress. The following is an example of what we might say if things are not getting better:

> *THERAPIST*: Well, it would appear that things have not
>   gotten better.
> *CLIENT*: I really don't think so.
> *THERAPIST*: Okay, well, what else do you think we need
>   to be talking about, or thinking about, in here
>   that will make a difference?
> *CLIENT*: I'm not sure.
> *THERAPIST*: Just to make sure we are on the same track,
>   remind me again what will be different when
>   these problems are solved.
> *CLIENT*: I'll just feel better.

THERAPIST: What will be different when you feel better?

CLIENT: You mean what will I do to feel better?

THERAPIST: No, let's not worry right this minute about *how* you will feel better; let's assume we can figure that out later. So once you are feeling better, what will you be doing differently?

CLIENT: I don't know and that's the problem. If I can't even answer this, how can things get better? *(Notice this passive language and the lack of clarity of her goal.)*

THERAPIST: Well, suppose you did have some idea of how you want things to be; what difference do you think that would make for you?

CLIENT: I would relax a little and not be so uptight.

THERAPIST: When you are able to relax more, what else will be different?

CLIENT: I could open up to other things.

THERAPIST: Like...

CLIENT: I think I would get unstuck and start to move on with my life. *(Now the client is talking about the future and how she wants things to be and she may be unstuck.)*

Work on another goal or stop meeting. When nothing is getting better we will often point out to our clients that it appears that what we are doing is not helping the situation and perhaps it would make sense to try something different. We will also state that continuing to do what we have been is not an option, because it has already proven itself to be non-effective. The following case example is the most typical scenario for this type of interaction with a client:

Case Example: Joan and Fred came to counseling to "improve communication." They have been married for six years, and have one child. During the first session Fred mentioned that he drinks now and then, and that Joan does not like it. Nothing further has been mentioned about the drinking until this, their fourth session.

> *THERAPIST*: Well, it seems to me that what we have been doing is not working. I do not think that it makes any sense to continue on in this manner if it is not going to help you.
>
> *JOAN*: Does this mean that we give up?
>
> *THERAPIST*: No, not at all. It means we have to take a second look at our work together.
>
> *FRED*: What do you mean?
>
> *THERAPIST*: Good question. Well, we have been talking a lot about your communication. You have tried several things to improve it and yet neither of you is reporting that the marriage is any better. I am curious about that.
>
> *FRED*: I can't explain it.
>
> *THERAPIST*: Do you think that there might be another goal that we need to work on before we can deal with your marital communication?
>
> *JOAN*: I do.
>
> *THERAPIST*: Is this something that you are comfortable saying in here?
>
> *JOAN*: I'm not sure, the last time I brought this up in therapy, we separated for three weeks and Fred gave me nothing but pure hell for months.
>
> *THERAPIST*: Well, then before you do discuss it, would you and Fred like to talk about it without me here?
>
> *FRED*: No, it's okay, she is talking about my drinking. She thinks I have a drinking problem.
>
> *THERAPIST*: Is that what you were going to say, Joan?
>
> *JOAN*: Yes, but not that politely (*all laugh*).
>
> *THERAPIST*: Fred, what is your view about your drinking?

FRED: I don't think it is a problem. I'm not an alcoholic or anything. I get to work on time and I don't hit my kid. Me and the boys just go drinking now and then.

JOAN: Most nights after work and on the weekends.

THERAPIST: Joan, what's your opinion on Fred's drinking?

JOAN: Well, before I tell you I want Fred to promise not to leave this time.

FRED: I won't, I really do want this (*the marriage*) to work.

JOAN: Okay, well, I hate when he drinks. He comes home late, sits down in front of the TV, and ignores us. I just want him to stop.

THERAPIST: So when he stops, what do you think will be different?

JOAN: What do you mean?

THERAPIST: When Fred's drinking is no longer a problem, what will be different?

JOAN: He won't come home late all the time.

THERAPIST: What else?

JOAN: He'll spend more time with the kids...

We will continue to ask questions until we have a clear goal; then we ask the progress scaling question and determine a next small step.

Coping questions. At times we have found it very useful to ask clients who do not seem to be getting better a series of questions called coping questions (Berg & Miller, 1993). As the name implies, we want to discover how it is that the client is managing to cope during this difficult time. We have found that these types of questions work very well with suicidal clients, severely depressed clients, and clients in acute crisis.

- *How is it that things are not worse?*
- *What have you done to keep things from getting worse?*
- *What would it take for you to say that things are a little bit better?*

- *When you are feeling like you are going to hurt yourself* [drink, yell], *how do you overcome the urge to do this?*
- *How long does it take for these feelings to go away?*
- *How do you get these feelings to go away?*
- *What have you done in the past to cope with this situation?*
- *What would it take for you to do this again?*

We ask all or some of these questions depending on the situation. This coping sequence is a piece of this model that can be integrated into any existing practice without changing other aspects of your practice. In fact, many crisis workers, on-call clinicians, and emergency room workers have been using this type of coping sequence for years.

Ultimately we would change therapists. If therapy continues for up to eight sessions and the client is still not reporting any change, we will consider changing therapists. Of course we discuss this fully with the client and ultimately it is up to the client, therapist, and insurance company whether to change therapists. Research indicates that the average number of sessions clients are in treatment is eight. This average is consistent across modalities and has remained the same over many years (Miller, 1993a). If the average is eight, and the client is not reporting any progress, it makes sense to try something more dramatic as the number of sessions approaches eight. We had one client who entered therapy despite the fact that being in therapy could jeopardize her job. This added more pressure to an already stressful situation. After six sessions, three team meetings, and trying various techniques in the session, the client and therapist decided to transfer the case to another therapist. When the managed care company was called, and we explained why we were requesting the change, the reviewer was pleased with our decision, approved the change, gave the new therapist six more sessions before the next review, and thanked us for doing her job.

Special clients. There are clients who have such severe conditions that no progress overall may be noticed during the course of a "brief" therapeutic encounter. These clients may be suffering from chronic pain or long-term depression. With these clients we have found it useful to concentrate on those times in their lives when they feel a little better and how they do that. We typically meet with this type of client over a greater period of time (assuming there is no or minimal risk of suicidal actions). We do, however, remain Solution Focused throughout the treatment. We concentrate on coping questions and what they do to make their lives just a little better. The goals are small, and validating our clients' continual pain or depression is an integral aspect of our work.

12

Integration

Pitfalls to avoid

Nylund and Corsiglia (1994) skillfully point out in their article "Becoming Solution-~~Focused~~ Forced in Brief Therapy" five pitfalls to avoid in Solution Focused Therapy. They state that the following will lead to "failed" therapy:

Don't acknowledge and validate the client's problem.

Do ask questions in an instrumental manner without adequate attunement to the emotional context, pacing of the interview or body language of the client.

Do argue for exceptions that don't make a difference to the client.

Do become the expert as the therapist and pursue your own goals, not the client's.

Don't create a therapeutic environment of curiosity, openness and respect. (Nylund and Corsiglia; 1994, p. 11)

There is an ongoing discussion to understand more fully what actually works in treatment (Lambert, 1992; Miller, Hubble, & Duncan, 1995). The therapeutic relationship appears to be one of the major factors leading to successful treatment (Miller, Hubble, & Duncan, 1995).

Making a diagnosis

In this era of managed behavioral health care, we are often required to give a diagnosis and formulate behavioral treatment goals after the first or second session. In order to be able to accomplish this, we add several tools to our first few encounters with our clients. Whenever possible we ask clients to fill out a form that lists some basic information before they arrive at our office. We call this form our Client Information Form. This reduces the need to gather some information during the first few sessions; we then add this information to the client's record. The client information form will vary depending on the agency's and/or state's requirements. Some of the information we now include is the following:

- Hospitalizations/surgeries
- Serious illness/injury including head trauma
- Chronic medical conditions
- Allergies
- Current prescriptions and medications
- Physician's name, address, phone number, date of last visit
- Family history: any major mental or physical health or drug/alcohol issues
- Prior therapy or counseling: name of therapist/counselor, dates seen, inpatient stays

- Any additional information that you feel is important.
- Goals the client hopes to achieve in treatment/counseling.
- Another section of this form is the problem list. On this part of the form we ask the client to identify any of the problems that he feels is currently affecting him or a significant other. (Note: The original model for this form was taken from the Brief Family Therapy Center in Milwaukee and has been expanded by several people, including ourselves. See Chapter 13).

It is the rare exception that we are unable to formulate a clinical diagnosis based on the client's response to the miracle question and the follow-up questions. Near the end of the session, right before we take our break, we will ask any questions that we need to in order to fill out any forms required by our agency, or any other information we feel is necessary. These can include

- Information needed to complete managed care forms for further authorization.
- Information about hallucinations, which typically is not discussed in a first session.
- Other questions to enable us to make a clear differential diagnosis and formulate behavioral treatment goals.
- Information we may need in order to make a psychiatric referral.

For example, when we needed to complete an Outpatient Treatment Report form for the HMO that was managing Renee's treatment (see end of Chapter 9), the initial goals of treatment were these:

Goal: Obtain a job.
Plan: First step is for client to go on two job interviews. This will be supported using Solution Focused Therapy.

Goal: Stabilize and improve overall mood as measured by increased organization.

Plan: Client will use Solution Focused scales to monitor mood throughout the day. Client will learn to connect improvement in mood to increased organization in her daily life.

There are several managed care companies that allow us to use V-codes from the DSM-IV for Axis I diagnoses. We have found that these often describe the problem as the client views it more accurately than other codes. There are many issues we consider when diagnosing clients that are not necessarily Solution Focused concerns but rather our own. Some diagnoses can follow a client for many years and interfere with health, life, and disability insurance (Sykes, 1995). We continue to give the diagnosis of "Major Depressive Disorder, Recurrent, with Psychotic Features" (DSM IV, 1994), but we think much harder about the diagnosis now that we are Solution Focused. Becoming Solution Focused has meant that we generally think about pathology only when we are diagnosing for managed care and other insurance.

Dealing with managed behavioral care companies

Since the proliferation of managed behavioral health (mental health and substance abuse), many therapists have struggled to find common ground with which to communicate effectively with case reviewers. We have found that the Solution Focused assumptions and techniques provide us with a highly effective means by which to negotiate with managed care. One of the keys to successfully dealing with managed care reviewers is to understand the reviewer's view of the world (as you would with a client) and work from there. It has been our experience that when we need to advocate for more sessions for our clients, and on that rare occasion ask for extended benefits or even flex benefits (the transfer of inpatient dollars to outpatient dollars), we meet little resistance. This is due to the fact that with the majority of the other cases we see, we operate well within the expectations (in regard to session number and outcome) of the managed care companies.

Psychoeducation

On occasion we decide to educate our clients about particular information. We often get asked in our trainings, "Is it okay for me to tell the client this?" For us the decision to educate is not "being Solution Focused", rather, it is based on our training as social workers. There are several topics that we have decided clients need to be informed about. We have debated long and hard as to what topics fall into this category. Some of these topics include domestic violence, availability of services for the poor, information on HIV and AIDS, and safe sex issues (particularly for sexually active adolescents). One of our roles as clinicians is being distributors of information, and being Solution Focused does not negate this responsibility. We encourage all clinicians to think about what topics they will chose to educate clients about. Clients will sometimes ask us our opinion on a particular topic. We gently explain to our clients that no matter what we would do in a given situation, that "solution" may not work for them, particularly since it has not come from their set of values. We also talk about not wanting people to become dependent on us to give them answers when they get stuck; rather, we would like to help them discover their own way of problem solving for the future.

Mandated reporting

There are other times when we will impose goals or our agenda onto the client. Being licensed social workers in Massachusetts means that we are mandated to report suspected abuse or neglect of a child, handicapped person, or elderly person. This is most often not the client's goal. The balance between being Solution Focused and gathering enough information to file a report of abuse is often difficult at best. We attempt to distinguish the counseling from the mandated reporting issues as best we can. One solution is to conduct a Solution Focused session and then at the end discuss the mandated reporting issues.

Taking responsibility for change

When clients report that things are better, we ask lots of questions about how the change has occurred. There are times when clients say they do not know, and we have heard other therapists describe this as clients "not taking responsibility." We, on the other hand, assume that clients truly do not either realize or believe they had anything to do with the change.

Machine-gunning the client

When first learning this model we found that we had a tendency to ask too many questions in a row, too fast, and not give the client an opportunity to think, let alone respond adequately. The session appeared more of a question-and-answer tennis match than a real conversation. In an effort to stop "machine gunning" questions at the client (and what else, and what else...) and begin to have a conversation, we found it useful to remember that we could only formulate our next question after listening to the client's response to the previous question. Most clinicians find it helpful to not worry too much about the order of the questions (since the order is not set in stone) and to concentrate on listening to our clients.

Remembering the parts of a session

When we first started doing Solution Focused Therapy, we found it difficult to remember the various parts of a session. One method we used until we became familiar and comfortable with the model was to go into the session with an outline (see outline of a session form in Chapter 13). Some clinicians have a difficult time remembering exception questions, and we recommend writing down several examples and taking them into a session.

When to begin using Solution Focused Therapy

We often get asked, "When should I try this? With whom?" Integrating the Solution Focused model into our clinical work took several months. We began by doing Solution Focused sessions with new clients. We also started trying some of the techniques, particularly scaling and looking for exceptions, with clients with whom we had been working for a while, and who were not reporting any progress. When integrating the Solution Focused model into our work we followed the assumptions of the model itself; if it works, do it more. With those clients with whom we were working who were reporting progress, we continued doing work in a similar manner. To do otherwise would be contrary to the model and confuse our clients. One use of the scaling questions with our ongoing clients was to determine if the client was making progress. This also helped us to clarify when to begin talking about termination with our clients. For these clients we also tried starting our sessions with, "What's been better?" This began to change both our and our clients' expectations that their lives should be getting better while being in therapy.

Over time we both decided that we were going to practice only Solution Focused Therapy. We are definitely the exception, not the rule. Over the years we have come into contact with only a handful of clinicians who have decided to exclusively practice in a Solution Focused manner. The vast majority of clinicians have integrated pieces of the model into their existing practice. We have taken the model and made it our own. If you were to see us do a session and then watch another Solution Focused therapist do a session, you would readily recognize that there are variances in how the model is practiced. One last word on this: We ask ourselves, before asking a question of a client, how asking the client that particular question will be helpful to our client's meeting *his* goals. If we are not sure that asking a particular question will be helpful toward meeting his goal, then we do not ask it.

With whom should this model not be used?

This is a vital question in the field of mental health. Unfortunately, at the present time, there exists very little, if any, good research that indicates for which clients this model works and does not work. In his article "The Solution Conspiracy, A Mystery in Three Installments," Dr. Scott Miller (1993a) discusses the lack of evidence concerning the efficacy of Solution Focused Therapy. What we have found is that it is most often the clinician for whom this model is not a good fit. As with any model of therapy, if the clinician is not comfortable with the assumptions of the model, then the questions will be just "techniques" and the therapy disingenuous and probably not effective. If we do not believe that a particular client will respond well to the miracle question, we do not ask it. In these cases we sometimes ask the alternative question, which sounds more concrete. There are some clients who do not like us when we are using the Solution Focused model (or they just don't like us). We expect that a percentage of our clients will not be comfortable with us or the model. We encourage our clients to tell us if the therapy is not working for them. We then try to find another therapist who may be a better fit.

Consultations, transfers and long-term clients

There are times when we are asked to do case consultations. Most often both the client(s) and therapist are feeling stuck. Other times a managed behavioral health care company will request we meet with a client, couple, or family, to get a second opinion. We typically will gather a larger team than normal to sit behind the mirror, and ask the client's therapist to be part of the team. We will often start these sessions by asking this scaling question developed by Steve deShazer (1994):

On a scale from 0 to 10, where 0 is when the problems that brought you to counseling were at their worst, and 10 is when they are solved enough that you do not need to be in therapy anymore, where would you say you are right now?

We would then ask several follow-up questions, assuming that the client's answer was above zero:

* *How did you go from a zero to a three?*
* *What did you do to get to a three?*
* *What about therapy helped with this change?*
* *What has your therapist done that has been helpful?*
* *What would need to happen for you to say that you are a 3.5?*

When clients have been in long-term therapy prior to seeing us, we feel care must be taken to validate their previous work. Oftentimes the number of sessions that the client will be in therapy with us will be significantly less than their prior experience in long-term therapy. Care should be taken in our opinion so that these clients do not feel that their time in longer-term treatment was ill spent. We often ask clients lots of questions about their past therapy:

- *What was helpful about your past therapy?*
- *How do you feel this was helpful?*
- *What did you do to get better?*
- *What did the therapist do that you found helpful?*
- *What did the therapist do that you did not find helpful?*

Working with mandated clients

Most therapists have to work with mandated clients, and clients that would rather be anywhere else than in your office. In our work with adolescents, many clients have told us that their goal is, "for you and everyone who looks like you to get out of my face!" The focus of our intervention is directed toward cooperating with the client, which decreases clients' "resistance."

> *THERAPIST*: So what brings you here today?
> *CLIENT:* I'm being forced to come.
> *THERAPIST*: So you don't think you need to be here?
> *CLIENT:* Of course not!
> *THERAPIST*: **So who do you need to convince that**
> **you don't need to be here anymore?**
> *CLIENT:* My parents I guess, and the guidance
> counselor.

When we agree with our clients' views of the world, and ask who they need to convince that they don't need therapy, (we make it clear that they do not need to convince us as the therapist), resistance and denial are greatly reduced (for a more in depth discussion see Tohn and Oshlag, 1996).

Working with systems

We often find ourselves using Solution Focused questions with other clinicians and service providers such as school personnel, probation officers, attorneys, and protective service workers. When doing collateral work, we use Solution Focused questions to discern what the client needs to do differently and how others involved in the client's life will know that these changes are occurring. Below is a typical example of a conversation we might have with a protective services worker:

THERAPIST: I was wondering if you could help me understand what Amy needs to accomplish in treatment in order for you to deem it successful.

WORKER: Well, she will learn how to be a good parent and then we might consider letting her have some time with her kids.

THERAPIST: When you say "good parent," can you give me some specifics so that I can share them with Amy?

WORKER: I don't want you to tell her what to do, because then she will just do it and think she can get her kids back.

THERAPIST: So is there more that she has to do than just be a good parent?

WORKER: Of course, I'm not even sure she could do anything to get her kids back at this point.

THERAPIST: Oh. Well, I would like to work on realistic goals with Amy and not set her up for a disappointment in the end. It sounds like you don't trust that Amy's changes will be long-lasting ones. Is that your concern?

WORKER: Well, yes. I see that all the time, and then the
kids suffer.

THERAPIST: The last thing any of us wants is for these
kids to suffer anymore. Let me ask you if you
have a sense of how long Amy would need to
maintain these changes in order for you to be
confident they were lasting changes and not just a
manipulative attempt to get her kids back.

WORKER: Well, I don't know. I haven't thought about
it that way.

THERAPIST: It would be helpful to me if you could give
this some thought, and we could talk about this
again before I meet with Amy in two weeks. Is
that something you have time for?

WORKER: Sure, I can think about it.

This line of questioning is asking the worker to set well-formed goals, and
the next conversation would get much more specific around behavioral
and measurable changes.

We also feel that it is important for clients to be involved in these
conversations. We will often ask the client to call or meet with or be part
of the meetings with these other service providers.

Multiple tasks

When there is more than one person in the room, we may give
different tasks to different people. For example, a client may be in the
customer-seller type relationship for one goal, but in the visitor-host
relationship for another goal. We would give a "do" task for the
customer-seller goal, and no task for the visitor-host goal.

Complicated tasks

When we first started doing Solution Focused Therapy we tended
to give very complicated tasks to our clients. Over time we have moved to

a much simpler version of task assignment as described in Chapter 9. When clients are not reporting progress, we have noticed a tendency to want to assign more complicated tasks. It is important to keep in mind that tasks are determined by several factors, and foremost is the client-therapist-goal relationship. Although there are some excellent guides to forming more complicated tasks (O'Hanlon & Weiner-Davis, 1989; deShazer, 1985; Molnar & deShazer, 1987), we try very hard to help our clients determine what will work best for them. There are times, however, that our clients just do not know what they could do to improve their situation and turn to us for suggestions. On rare occasions we will be more directive in assigning a task.

Solution Focused Therapy is not for everyone

We have found that Solution Focused Therapy does not work for every clinician, nor for every client. As Scott Miller (1993a) points out, the model does not produce a different therapeutic outcome from other forms of therapy, but what we do during the session is different. If this were *the therapy*, we would all already be practicing it! It would be unwise to strictly adhere to any one model of therapy given that it does not work for every therapist, nor for every client. At the present time more research needs to be done to determine with whom this model does not work. From examining our own work, we have found no correlation between those times that the model does not work (read: client reports no progress) and such factors as age, sex, presenting problem, diagnosis, treatment modality (individual, family, couple, group), or setting (private practice, community outpatient, inpatient, partial hospitalization). Based on our anecdotal research we have found that most clinicians choose to do a certain type of therapy because it fits their personality. Clients choose a therapist based on the therapist's personality and the rapport established over the phone or by the end of the first session.

Some of our trainees have told us that in order to practice Solution Focused Therapy they have had to "give up" asking about the problem to the degree they were accustomed to and reel in their voyeuristic tendencies. Some seasoned clinicians have compared learning this model to learning a new language. Everything we say we question anew. For many this process can be an exhilarating challenge. Making this transition is not for everyone. When we encounter clinicians who are uncomfortable using Solution Focused Therapy, we encourage them to explore one of the other forms of brief therapy until they find one that is comfortable for them.

Don't confuse the client

Although it was stated earlier, it warrants repeating: For those clients who are reporting progress, it would be confusing, and potentially interfering, for you to switch treatment methods in the middle of a treatment episode. We recommend using the model with new clients, clients who are reporting no progress, and clients with whom you are feeling stuck.

It's not a cookbook!

Although we have presented the material in a particular order, sessions do not necessarily proceed in this fashion. We encourage clinicians to listen to their clients. We have found that our clients are very good at leading us to the next question that will help them reach their goal. It is perfectly fine to sit in silence and think about your next question. When the model is used in a cookbook type fashion it appears cold, calculated, and not very effective; start with rapport. There will be sessions in which you do not ask the miracle question, start with scaling or exceptions, or do the whole session in a unique order. Being Solution Focused is a way of being with clients, not an order to your intervention questions.

Seeing a live session

It is one thing to read about and practice Solution Focused Therapy; however, the most powerful learning tool we have found to date is watching live and taped sessions. Most likely there is at least one Solution Focused therapist practicing in your area. One way to find out who offers supervision and/or who utilizes the team approach and will allow you to be part of a team is to call us. You can also consult *News of the Difference* (D. Simon, ed.), which includes a listing of Solution Focused clinicians and their locales at the end of each issue.

Practice, practice, practice

We worked very hard to learn Solution Focused Therapy. We practiced with each other, and many other clinicians and clients, before feeling comfortable and making the model our own. We have made changes to the model as we have practiced it, and it now fits our personalities. We invite you to try it and see what difference it makes for you.

Last Words

Working in a Solution Focused manner can be exhilarating. As the increased demand for more focused and briefer clinical work continues, clinicians must continue to search to discover what works, and what does not.

13

Forms

We have included several forms that we hope are useful as you begin to integrate Solution Focused Therapy into your clinical work. Feel free to copy these and use them. The forms include the following:

Client information form: This is sent to the client prior to the first session, when possible. This form should be altered to meet your agency's and/or states' needs. Remember that certain behavioral health care companies require you to gather specific history.

First session form: To be used when meeting with a client for the first time as a reminder of the various questions. This form was given to us, along with the second session form, by Larry Hopwood in 1991.

Later session form: To be used as a guide for later sessions.

Progress notes: This is the form we fill out and enter into our records.

All of these forms are available from the authors on diskette for a minimal fee. They can be converted into most popular software languages. Some are forms we merely print for use in a session, and others have built in macros for automation. For more information on computer forms, please contact the authors.

CLIENT INFORMATION

Please provide the information requested below. This is confidential
information and will not be released to anyone without written permission from
the client.

NAME: _____

Medical History: Please give a brief statement regarding:

1. Hospitalizations/Surgeries: _____

2. Serious Illness/Injury (including head injuries): _____

3. Chronic Medical Conditions (include allergies): _____

4. Current Prescriptions/ Medications: _____

5. Physician's Name: _____ Date of Last Visit: _____
Physician's Telephone Number: _____

6. Family History: Any major mental or physical health or drug/alcohol issues.
_____
_____

Client Information Form
Page 2

Problems that you feel apply to you and/or a significant other (please indicate whom the problem refers to):

___ Depression	___ Alcohol/Other Drug Abuse (Self)
___ Suicidal Thoughts	___ Alcohol/Other Drug Abuse (Family)
___ Suicidal Actions	___ Marital/Relationship Problems
___ Anxiety	___ Sexual Problems
___ Panic Attacks	___ Career Choice Concerns
___ Sleep Problems	___ Sexual Abuse, Actual or Threatened
___ Eating Disorder	___ Physical Abuse
___ Withdrawn Behavior	___ Family Violence, Actual or Threatened
___ Job-Related Problems	___ Death of Loved One
___ Financial Concerns	___ Compulsive Gambling
___ Parent-Child Conflict (Self)	___ Self-Esteem
___ Parent-Child Conflict (Spouse)	___ School Problems
___ Parent-Child Conflict (Both)	___ Brother/Sister Problems
___ Communication Problems	___ Blended Family Issues
___ Running Away	___ Parental Loss of Control
___ Other	___ Legal Difficulties

Prior Therapy or Counseling

_____

Name of Therapist/Counselor: Dates Seen:

_____   _____

Please provide any additional information that you feel is important.

_____

Please list the goals you hope to achieve in treatment/counseling (be specific).

_____

FIRST SESSION

Name of Client: _____ Date: _____

History and Complaint:

Goals:

Miracle:

Exceptions:

Scaling: Progress (next step)
        Willingness
        Confidence

Intervention Message:

Plan:

LATER SESSION

Name of Client: _____ Date: _____

Goals:

What's Better:

Scale: (Last Time __):

Next Step:

Intervention Message:

Plan:

PROGRESS NOTES

Client Name: Client Number:
Therapist:
Session:
Number of Authorized Sessions Remaining:
Date:
Present at Session:
Team Members:

Goals Worked On:

Progress:

New Goals:

Scaling:

Intervention Message:

Notes:

Plan:

_____   _____
Signature of Clinician   Date

References

American Psychiatric Association (1994). *Diagnostic and Statistical Manual of Mental Disorders (Fourth Edition)*. Washington, DC: American Psychiatric Association.

Berg, I. K. (1991). *Family Based Services: A Solution-Focused Approach*. Milwaukee: BFTC Press.

Berg, I. K., & Miller, S. (1992). *Working with the Problem Drinker: A Solution-Focused Approach*. New York: W. W. Norton and Company.

Brasher, B., Campbell, T., & Moen, D., (1993). Solution Oriented Recovery. *Journal of Systemic Therapies,* 12(3), 1-14.

Budman, S., Hoyt, M., & Friedman, S.(1992). *The First Session in Brief Therapy*. New York: Guilford Press.

Cain, H., & Markowski, E. (1993). The Flip Chart as Greek Chorus. *Journal of Systemic Therapies*, 12(3), 44-49.

Cameron-Bandler, L. (1985). *Solutions: Practical and Effective Antidotes for Sexual and Relationship Problems*. San Rafael, CA: FuturePace.

Carroll, L. (1988). *Alice's Adventures in Wonderland*. New York: Knopf.

Coale, H. (1992). The Constructivist Emphasis on Language: A Critical
    Conversation. *Journal of Strategic and Systemic Therapies*,
    11(1), 12-23.

Dawes, R. (1994). *House of Cards: Psychology and Psychotherapy Built
    on Myth*. New York: The Free Press.

deShazer, S. (1985). *Keys to Solution in Brief Therapy*. New York:
    W. W. Norton and Company.

deShazer, S. (1988). *Clues: Investigating Solutions in Brief Therapy*.
    New York: W. W. Norton.

deShazer, S. (1989). Resistance Revisited. *Contemporary Family Therapy*,
    11(4) (Winter), 227-233.

deShazer, S. (1994). *Words Were Originally Magic*. New York: W. W.
    Norton and Company.

deShazer, S., Berg, I., Lipchik, E., Nunnally, E., Molnar, A., Gingerich,
    W., & Wiener-Davis, M. (1986). Brief Therapy: Focused
    Solution-Development. *Family Process* (25), 207-222.

Dolan, Y. (1991). *Resolving Sexual Abuse: Solution Focused Therapy
    and Ericksonian Hypnosis for Adult Survivors*. New York:
    W. W. Norton and Company.

Efron, J., Lukens, R., & Lukens, M., (1988). Constructivism: What's in it
    for you. *Family Therapy Networker*, 12(5), 26-35.

Epston, D. (1994). Extending the Conversation. *Family Therapy
    Networker* (Nov/Dec.), 30-37, 62-63.

Fischer, K. (1984). *Human Development: From Conception Through
    Adolescence*. New York: W. H. Freeman and Company.

Friedman, S., & Fanger, M.(1991). *Expanding Therapeutic Possibilities.* New York: Macmillan.

Gallagher, D. (1992). When Not Is Not a Knot. *News of the Difference,* 1(1), 9-11.

Hudson, P., & O'Hanlon, W. (1991). *Rewriting Love Stories: Brief Marital Therapy.* New York: W. W. Norton and Company.

Jensen, E. (1988) *Super-Teaching: Master Strategies for Building Student Success.* Del Mar, CA: Turning Point for Teachers.

Lambert, M. J. (1992). Implication of outcome research for psychotherapy integration. In J. C. Norcross & M. R. Goldfried (eds.), *Handbook of Psychotherapy Integration.* New York: Basic Books.

Lipchik, E. (1994). The Rush to Be Brief. *Family Therapy Networker* (March/April), 34-39.

Miller, S. (1992a). The Symptoms of Solutions. *Journal of Strategic and Systemic Therapies,* 11(1), 1-11.

Miller, S. (1992b). Personal communication.

Miller, S. (1993a). The Solution Conspiracy, A Mystery in Three Installments. *Journal of Strategic and Systemic Therapies,* 13(1), 18-37.

Miller, S. (1993b). Joint Workshop in Boston, MA.

Miller, S., & Hopwood, L. (1994). The Solution Papers: A Comprehensive Guide to the Publications of the Brief Family Therapy Center. *Journal of Systemic Therapies,* 13(1), 42-47.

Miller, S., Hubble, M., & Duncan, B. (1995). No More Bells and Whistles. *Family Therapy Networker* (March/April), 53-63.

Miller, S., Hubble, M., & Duncan, B. (1996). *Handbook of Solution-Focused Brief Therapy.* San Francisco: Jossey-Bass.

Miller, S., Hubble, M., & Duncan, B. (1997). *Escape from Babel: Toward a Unifying Language for Psychotherapy Practice.* New York: W. W. Norton and Company.

Molnar, A., & deShazer, S. (1987). Solution-Focused Therapy: Toward the Identification of Therapeutic Tasks. *Journal of Marital and Family Therapy*, 13(4), 349-358.

Nylund, D., & Corsiglia, V. (1994). Becoming Solution-~~Focused~~ Forced in Brief Therapy: Remembering Something Important We Already Knew. *Journal of Systemic Therapies*, 13(1), 5-12.

O'Hanlon, W. (1994). The Third Wave. *Family Therapy Networker,* (Nov/Dec.), 18-29.

O'Hanlon, W., & Martin, M. (1992). *Solution-Oriented Hypnosis; An Eriksonian Approach.* New York: W. W. Norton and Company.

O'Hanlon, W., & Weiner-Davis, M. (1989). *In Search of Solutions: A New Direction in Psychotherapy.* New York: W. W. Norton and Company.

O'Hanlon, W., & Wilk, J. (1987). *Shifting Contexts: The Generation of Effective Psychotherapy.* New York: Guilford Press.

Rabkin, R. (1983). *Strategic Psychotherapy.* New York: Meridian.

Ray, C., & Oss, M.(1993). *Community Mental Health and Managed Care Managed Mental Health Care*, San Francisco: Jossey-Bass.

Rossi, E. L. (1973). Psychological Shocks and Creative Moments in Psychotherapy. *American Journal of Clinical Hypnosis*, 16(1), 9-22.

Smith, T., Yoshioka, M., & Winton, M.(1993). A Qualitative Understanding of Reflecting Teams I: Client Perspectives. *Journal of Systemic Therapies*, 12(3), 28-43.

Talmon, M. (1990). *Single Session Therapy; Maximizing the Effect of the First (and Often Only) Therapeutic Encounter*. San Francisco: Jossey-Bass.

Tomm, K., & Lannamann, J. (1988). Questions As Interventions. *Family Therapy Networker*, 12(5), 38-41.

Tohn, S. & Oshlag, J. (1996). Solution-Focused Therapy with Mandated Clients: Cooperating with the Uncooperative. In S. Miller, M. Hubble, & B. Duncan (Eds.), *Handbook of Solution-Focused Brief Therapy*. San Francisco: Jossey-Bass.

Walter, J., & Peller, J. (1992). *Becoming Solution-Focused in Brief Therapy*. New York: Brunner-Mazel.

Watzlawick, P., Weakland, J., & Fisch, R.(1974). *Change: Principals of Problem Formation and Problem Resolution*, New York: W. W. Norton and Company.

Weiner-Davis, M., deShazer, S., & Gingerish, W. (1987). Building on Pretreatment Change to Construct the Therapeutic Solution: An Exploratory Study. *Journal of Marital and Family Therapy*, 13(4), 359-363.

Wylie, M. S. (1994). Endangered Species. *Family Therapy Networker* (March/April), 20-33.

Wylie, M. S., (1995). Diagnosing for Dollars? *Family Therapy Networker* (May/June), 23-33, 65-69.

Further Resources

Family Therapy Networker, Richard Simon, editor. Subscription
     Services, 8528 Bradford Road, Silver Spring, MD 20901. (301)
     589-6536.

Journal of Systemic Therapies, Don Efron and Harlene Anderson, co-
     senior editors.   Guilford Publications, 72 Spring Street, New
     York, NY 10012. (800) 365-7006.

News of the Difference, Dvorah Simon, editor. 392 CPW #20 U, New
     York, NY 10025. (212) 662-4950.

Solutions, 243 Hudson Road, Sudbury, MA. 01776-1624. (508) 443-
     7574. Internet: sltjao@sprynet.com

Author Index

Subject Index